T0311915

The Anthropocene

This book introduces the concept of the Anthropocene and examines its importance for environmental legal thinking, research and practice. Two main arguments are explored. The first is that much of the scholarship in environmental law that addresses the Anthropocene does not respond to Earth systems science or the difference in scale as we move from local to global systems. Key examples include a focus on anthropocentrism, attempts to constitutionalise environmental protections, the prevalence of legal rights and the idea of ecological integrity. The second argument is that these points of focus derive from the prevalence of idealism in environmental legal scholarship. Idealism in this context does not refer to naivety or the presentation of unrealistic goals. Rather, this book is concerned with idealism as a philosophical commitment to the power of ideas to determine reality and drive future change. As expressed in legal scholarship, this book also argues that idealism involves an abstraction from material reality and a refusal to directly engage those forces that have given rise to the Anthropocene. In response, this book uses a method of critique to uncover the presumptions and presuppositions that underlie environmental scholarship. As a counter to idealism, it also sketches out a framework for materialism in the Anthropocene.

This book's engagement with these questions will appeal to undergraduate and postgraduate students in law, politics, philosophy or the ecological humanities. It will also be of interest to academics in these disciplines and libraries around the world.

Peter D. Burdon is Associate Professor at Adelaide Law School, University of Adelaide, Australia.

Part of the NEW TRAJECTORIES IN LAW series

series editors

Adam Gearey, Birkbeck College, University of London
Prabha Kotiswaran, Kings College London
Colin Perrin, Commissioning Editor, Routledge
Mariana Valverde, University of Toronto

for information about the series and details of previous and forthcoming titles, see https://www.routledge.com/New-Trajectories-in-Law/book-series/NTL

A GlassHouse Book

The Anthropocene

New Trajectories in Law

Peter D. Burdon

Routledge
Taylor & Francis Group
a GlassHouse Book

First published 2023
by Routledge
4 Park Square, Milton Park, Abingdon, Oxon OX14 4RN

and by Routledge
605 Third Avenue, New York, NY 10158

Routledge is an imprint of the Taylor & Francis Group, an informa business

a GlassHouse book

British Library Cataloguing-in-Publication Data
A catalogue record for this book is available from the British Library

ISBN: 978-0-367-48665-5 (hbk)
ISBN: 978-1-032-53742-9 (pbk)
ISBN: 978-1-003-41337-0 (ebk)

DOI: 10.4324/9781003413370

Typeset in Bembo
by Deanta Global Publishing Services, Chennai, India

Contents

Acknowledgements

This book had a long gestation period and was prolonged by the pandemic and associated impacts on the University sector. I want to thank Colin Perrin for writing to me with the idea for this book and for his great patience for the time it took for me to deliver the manuscript. Thank you also to Naomi Round Cahalin for her editorial assistance.

This book was written while I was on sabbatical from the University of Adelaide. I would like to thank the institution for supporting me to take leave so that I could complete this book without teaching and administrative responsibilities.

My family has been an unwavering source of support and love. Thank you to Shani, Freyja and Arlo for being my foundation and source of inspiration. You are examples of the best things in life, and I am grateful we get to spin around the sun together.

Parts of Chapters 2, 4 and 5 draw on arguments first adumbrated in journal articles. Part of Chapters 2 and 5 were first published in "Ecological law in the Anthropocene" 11(1–2) (2020) *Transnational Legal Theory*: 33–46. Part of Chapter 4 was first published in "Obligations in the Anthropocene" 31(3) (2020) *Law and Critique*: 309–328. Permission has been gained from Springer (https://www.springer.com) and Taylor & Francis Group (https://www.tandfonline.com/) to re-publish extracts. In both instances, the arguments have been updated, revised and placed into the context of this book.

Chapter 1

The Anthropocene Rupture

This short book contains two central arguments. The first is that much of the scholarship in environmental law[1] that addresses the Anthropocene does so using concepts derived from the Holocene which are no longer fit for purpose. By this I mean that they do not respond to Earth systems science or the difference in scale as we move from local to global systems. Key examples which I engage include a focus on anthropocentrism, attempts to constitutionalise environmental protections, the prevalence of legal rights and the idea of ecological integrity. My second and more challenging argument is that the limitations I identify derive from the prevalence of idealism in legal scholarship. By idealism I do not mean naivety or the presentation of unrealistic goals. Rather, I am concerned with idealism as a philosophical commitment to the power of ideas to determine reality and drive future change. As expressed in legal scholarship, I also argue that idealism involves an abstraction from material reality and a refusal to directly engage those forces that have given rise to the Anthropocene.

To make this argument, the dominant method in this book is critique. For me, critique is a forward-looking practice that is aimed at uncovering the presumptions that underpin a concept or practice. Its intention is to help us see clearly and I think it is particularly generative when used to engage ideas that have the status of conventional wisdom. As is the case in every discipline, environmental legal scholarship has its own orthodoxy which proponents can put forward as a priori presuppositions. For me the Anthropocene represents an opportunity to test and, where necessary, rethink ideas that no longer serve us at this historical moment.

While the heart of this book is occupied with critique, I will also put forward positive proposals for environmental legal scholarship. For example, while I point to the limits of idealism as a politics, I don't discount the relevance of our mental conceptions of the world. For this reason, I propose new ways of thinking about anthropocentrism and propose a focus on legal obligations. I also argue that the Anthropocene lends itself

DOI: 10.4324/9781003413370-1

to an ethics that is ordered around human beings and is grounded in material reality. To this end, the conclusion of this book sets out what a materialist approach to environmental legal scholarship might entail and the various components of analysis that can help us think outside the strictures of idealism.

The remainder of this introduction establishes some foundational points upon which my argument is built. Because of the centrality of the Anthropocene to this project, I begin by thinking about the relationship between science and law and tracing some of the basic concepts in Earth systems science. Following this I provide a fuller outline of my argument and signpost the chapters that make up his book.

Environmental Law and Ecology

Since its inception environmental law has taken inspiration from the ecological sciences.[2] The term "inspiration" is deliberately chosen to reflect the fact that nature does not offer prescriptions. This reflects David Hume's contention (also known as Hume's law) that one cannot derive "ought" from "is" (1960: 469). Whatever steps we have taken to protect the environment have been motivated by additional reasons such as our desire to survive and flourish and have empathy for non-human animals. Environmental lawyers have offered interpretations of ecological science which are grounded in value judgements and choices. This in itself is not a critique. Any environmental lawyer worthy of the name would struggle to offer anything more than that and it would be dishonest to argue that one has derived an objective legal prescription from nature.

As is commonly stated, the word ecology derives from the ancient Greek οἶκος (oikos), meaning house or home. However, we can stretch the original Greek further to incorporate the idea of belonging to a family of kin or intimates (Liddell and Scott 2005: 477) and a place where divinity dwells in the natural world (Diggle 2021: 992). One of the first scientific statements of this term came from English botanist Arthur Tansley in 1935. Tansley resisted interpretations that imputed anthropomorphic or familial ideas onto the environment. He grounded his research in hard science and spoke about how energy and chemicals moved through living things (Nash 1989: 57).[3] Instead of describing these processes in terms of a biotic community, Tansley used the word "ecosystem." The name stuck and was developed further by a host of ecologists that included Eugene and Howard Odum (1953) and David Gates (1973).

These pioneers were grappling for language to describe the mutually dependent relationship they observed between living things, non-living matter and solar energy. Very quickly, policy makers took hold of these descriptions of fact and sought to draw out ethical implications. According to Nash (1989: 58), the first attempt was made with respect to policies on culling large predators such as "wolves, coyotes, mountain lions, bears, and even eagles and prairie dogs." In response, advocates like Charles Adams argued that large predators had a right to exist, and human beings needed to find a way to coexist with them (Nash 1989: 58). For Adams, the term "right" was a moral claim that was grounded in the value of non-human animals and the instrumental function they served as apex-predators in an ecosystem.[4] We are accustomed to such arguments today, but it should be stressed that Adams was presenting a new kind of argument that was distinct from purely anthropocentric justifications for environmental protection.

Human superiority was challenged further by the ecological concept of interdependence.[5] William Wheeler was an early proponent of this idea (Nash 1989: 59). His research into ants and termites led him to argue that there existed "an inexplicable 'social' tendency for wholes to combine … with wholes to form wholes of higher orders." Wheeler argued that this could be observed at the molecular level and in the social formation of complex organisms such as human beings. Wheeler (1926: 434) described this as an ecological community and argued that it created bonds of mutual dependence amongst the constituent parts. Here again we see a slippage from a description of fact and into a moral claim. This is more pronounced in thinkers like Alfred Emerson (1946: 9) who argued that ecological insights into interdependence could provide "a scientific basis for ethics."[6]

Such statements reflect a common tension with early approaches to environmental law and ethics – that is the extent to which they violated Hume's law noted above. We can see the tension here more clearly we if look more closely at environmental thinkers like Aldo Leopold who is arguably the most important theorist for first wave environmental legal thinking.[7] Leopold's seminal *A Sand Country Almanac* is explicit in drawing ethical prescriptions from ecology. "All ethics," he argues, "rest upon a single premise: that the individual is a member of a community of interdependent parts" (Leopold 1949: 203). This is an organic conception of nature and it proposes that every part has value and contributes to the good of the whole.

Leopold developed this idea further with his statement on the land ethic. In articulating this ethic, Leopold adopts the authority of an ecologist[8] and argues that human beings need to shift their perspective from conquerors of the land to "plain members and citizens of it." Ecology, in this interpretation, is a leveller and requires human beings to "respect" all parts of the land community. With reference to Hume's law we might break his argument into the following syllogism:

(i)   The environment is an interconnected whole;
(ii) Human beings are part of the environment;
(iii) Human beings *ought* to behave in a manner that respects the land community.

The problem with Leopold's reasoning is that the conclusion contains a copula not contained in the premises, namely, "ought." While we might regard Leopold's advice as sensible and prudent he has missed a critical step in logical deduction. Peter Singer (1981: 79) provides a useful illustration:

> the fact that the bull is charging does not, by itself, entail the recommendation: "Run!" It is only against the background of my presumed desire to live that the recommendation follows. If I intend to commit suicide in a manner that my insurance company will think an accident, no such recommendation applies.

So too with Leopold's argument. His conclusion only follows against a backdrop of assumptions that include our desire to live and flourish as part of a broader Earth community. There are evidently plenty of people who do not subscribe to this view. This includes tech billionaires planning to colonise Mars (Shaw 2021) and those promoting an ethic of radical individualism and self-sufficiency (Garrett 2020). The truth remains that facts have no direction, and their interpretation must be contested in the public sphere.

Subsequent writers have sought to overcome this problem by reading Leopold as a natural law theorist (Engel 2010: 35; Rolston 1989). This approach side steps Hume's law because advocates of natural law derive normative conclusions from moral facts (Shapiro 2011: 48). Following this line of reasoning, Leopold's (1949: 263) injunction that human beings "exercise the same constraints on our relation to the other members of the land community – soils, waters, plants and animals – as we do in our relation to other people" could be interpreted as a moral fact that completes his syllogism. This is a neat solution; however, it ignores the fact that Leopold never identified as a natural law thinker in any of his writings or public statements. For my purpose it is also desirable to ground environmental thinking in a more defensible theory of morality and law.[9]

Alongside statements of respect, Leopold also promoted the more radical idea that all components of an ecosystem have intrinsic rights. For example, Leopold (1949: 204) argued that soil and water had the "right to continued existence." This was not a utilitarian or an instrumental argument. Instead, Leopold (1949: 209) argued that all parts of an ecosystem should be allowed to thrive "as a matter of biotic right, regardless of the presence or absence of economic advantage to us." In this sense, existence determines whether an entity has intrinsic value and human beings are encouraged to see ourselves, not as unique but as an equal part of a greater whole. In more concrete terms, Leopold (1949: 211) argues that humans have "obligations to land over and above those dictated by self-interest."

This notion of a biotic right was "intellectual dynamite" for environmental lawyers and philosophers (Nash 1989: 70). A host of new possibilities emerged, including legislation that recognised the intrinsic value of nature and placed obligations on human conduct (Bosselmann and Tarlock 1993–1994). To develop and interpret these concepts, ecological scientists were also brought before legislators and judges (Turgut 2008: 119). Alongside these applications there developed a radical idea that nature should be considered a legal subject, capable of holding rights. It is not necessary to provide a descriptive summary of how this argument developed from the 1970s.[10] However, arguably the most important writer to advocate for rights of nature was Christopher D. Stone (1972, 2010). Like Leopold, Stone's ethical worldview was saturated in ecological thinking (Nash 1989: 85). However, in the 30 years that separate Leopold and Stone, ideas like interconnectedness and mutual dependence had become normalised amongst environmental thinkers. Stone writes with those assumptions in place and focuses on the moral and legal requirements for expanding legal rights to include "forests, oceans, rivers and other so-called 'natural objects' in the environment – indeed, to the natural environment as a whole" (1972: 456). His argument also draws explicitly on past liberation struggles and how anthropocentrism has diminished our ability to see nature as anything but a resource for human exploitation. This leads Stone to ponder the conditions upon which those with privilege can see an entity as a subject, worthy of legal rights:

> The fact is, that each time there is a movement to confer rights onto some new "entity," the proposal is bound to sound odd or frightening or laughable. This is partly because until the rightless thing receives its rights, we cannot see it as anything but a thing for the use of "us" – those who are holding rights at the time.
>
> (Stone 1972: 455)

In this passage, Stone is trying to imagine a legal arrangement in which nature is regarded as a legal person. While his argument is grounded in ecology, he also puts those ideas into conversation with Lockean social philosophy and American liberalism to argue for an expanded conception of community. This leads to several noteworthy arguments such as suggesting that the State of Alaska should have more congressional representatives because of "all those trees and acres, those waterfalls and forests" (1972: 487). And lest readers respond with incredulity, Stone (1972: 487) reminds them that the United States political system "once counted each slave, as three-fifths of a man." Nature, according to Stone's ecological worldview, deserved at least as much.

It took over 30 years for Stone's argument to gain some traction in law. However, since 2006 we have witnessed a gradual expansion of rights at all levels of government (Burdon 2010; Burdon and Williams 2016; Boyd 2017). For many advocates of Earth Jurisprudence, rights are the natural expression of an eco-centric worldview law (Cullinan 2011; Berry 2006).[11] More generally, rights-talk has proliferated through instruments such as environmental human rights to become one of the most dominant forms of environmental expression in law. I will return to discuss legal rights and their relationship to ecology in Chapter 4. For now, it is sufficient to note that environmental lawyers and lawmakers have seen rights as an appropriate expression of ecological thinking. More generally, both have explicitly drawn on ecological science to think about how human communities ought to respond to environmental harm and its impact on the community.

Earth Systems Science

In the previous section I argued that environmental lawyers have drawn on the ecological sciences during the growth and development of environmental law. My intention has not been to evaluate those responses but simply to note the source of inspiration. This point is important for my argument because I also contend that scholars have often failed to engage with Earth systems science when thinking about how we might respond to the Anthropocene.[12] Instead, as Jeremy Davies (2016: 41) has argued, the term has "picked up a variety of incompatible meanings." For example, we can note instances where writers have treated the Anthropocene as a synonym for environmental harm.[13] Erle Ellis, for example, has argued that current changes to the Earth system are merely a continuation of the environmental crisis (2013: 32–35).[14] In similar terms, scholars who invoke Latour's (2017: 3) "new climactic regime" sometimes slip into reducing the Anthropocene as a place-holder for climate change (Matthews 2021: 33).[15] Other writers treat the Anthropocene as a cultural concept which can be engaged without "its scientific trappings" (Purdy 2015: 16). And it is not difficult to locate examples where environmental lawyers respond to the Anthropocene using concepts and frameworks developed in response to ecology. In some cases, this is a conscious attempt to stretch ecological law to the new object of inquiry (Garver 2021; Kotze 2017) while other examples appear to dissolve any distinction with the Holocene (Robinson 2020).

In this book I am primarily interested in the Anthropocene as a scientific concept. In making this choice I am not seeking to invalidate the various cultural and social scientific uses of the term. Nor am I seeking to portray the scientific interpretation as neutral and purely objective (Yusoff 2018). Instead, I follow Hamilton (2018: 10) in contending that, whatever debates surround the Anthropocene, "an understanding of the basic science must come first." This is particularly relevant to my argument, which is calling on environmental lawyers to engage seriously with Earth systems science when formulating new and creative responses to the Anthropocene.

Taking this perspective also provides some justification for using the term Anthropocene rather than the proliferation of alternatives such as the Capitalocene (Moore 2015; Malm 2015), Pyrocene (Pyne 2021) or Technocene (Nancy 2015). It is not that I don't accept the critique offered by these perspectives – as I will demonstrate in the chapters that follow, I worry deeply about the ways the term universalises responsibility and "erases histories of racism that were incubated through the regulatory structure of geologic relations" (Yusoff 2018: 10).[16] However, the term "Anthropocene" is here to stay[17] and we are at some distance from an agreed alternative. Social scientists will continue to critique the term and draw attention to the forces that gave rise to the new epoch, but as Hamilton (2018: 28) observes, "it is the scientists addressing the International Commission on Stratigraphy whose role it is to name divisions in the Geological Time scale, including the Holocene's successor."[18] Ultimately we need a term that does not purport to be neutral but is robust enough to hold the scientific meaning *and* the critiques that draw out points of erasure and inequity.

With that said we can now unpack the basic elements of Earth systems science that give rise to the Anthropocene.[19] The most succinct statement is provided by Hamilton (2018: 9) who describes the Anthropocene as a "recent rupture in Earth history arising from the impact of human activity on the Earth System as a whole." There is a lot to unpack in this pithy statement. Starting with the term "recent" I note that a lot of ink has been spilled on the origins of the Anthropocene. Moreover, as Daniel Matthews (2021: 23) has noted, the period "one favours lends itself to distinct political narratives and commitments." For example, those dating the Anthropocene to the beginnings of agriculture (Ruddiman 2003) tend to view the Anthropocene as an extension of human influence over the environment (Angus 2016: 54). Those dating from the colonial period and the movement of people and plants into new ecosystems (Lewis and Maslin 2015) draw attention to patterns of violence which are materially connected environmental and social inequities today. And those dating from the industrial revolution focus on the rise of industrial capitalism and profit motive as coercing a much more intensive plundering of the environment (Moore 2015; Malm 2015).

For the purpose of this book, the precise starting date is not a matter of substance.[20] Following the current consensus, I date the Anthropocene from the 1950s (Angus 2016: 38–47)[21] – what Will Steffen (2015a) and colleagues have called the "great acceleration." However, it is important to stress that none of my arguments turn on this decision. Commenting on the post-war period, Steffen and colleagues (2004: 131) note:

> One feature stands out as remarkable. The second half of the twentieth century is unique in the entire history of human existence on Earth. Many human activities reached take-off points sometime in the twentieth century and have accelerated sharply toward the end of the century. The last 50 years have without doubt seen the most rapid transformation of the human relationship with the natural world in the history of humankind.

The Anthropocene is also recent in the sense that we have only studied the Earth as a system since the 1980s.[22] Prior to this we could grasp aspects of the Earth system through systems modelling and Arctic ice-core drilling (Hamilton 2018: 10–11; Angus 2016: 29–38). The study of the Earth systems required new technology, such as satellites capable of gathering data around the world and computers that could analyse and transmit that information (Angus 2016: 30).

One of the earliest bodies to begin processing and analysing this data was the International Geosphere Biosphere Program (IGBP), which was initiated by the International Council of Scientific Unions in 1986. Drawing on this research, Frank Oldfield and Will Steffen provided the first sophisticated definition of the Earth system. Here is an extract: "the Earth System has come to mean the suite of interacting physical, chemical, and biological global-scale cycles (often called biogeochemical cycles) and energy fluxes which provide the conditions necessary for life on the planet" (Oldfield and Steffen 2004: 7). The Earth system also incorporates the metabolism of industrial culture. As the authors note:

> Human beings, their societies and their activities are an integral component of the Earth system, and are not an outside force perturbing an otherwise natural system. There are many modes of natural variability and instability within the System as well as anthropogenically driven changes. By definition, both parts of variability are part of the dynamics of the Earth System. They are often impossible to separate completely and they interact in complex and sometimes mutually reinforcing ways.
>
> (Oldfield and Steffen 2004: 7)

This definition has ideas in common with those articulated in ecology. For example, it articulates our profound connection with and ability to influence the health and functioning of living systems. And yet it is important to draw distinctions. Ecology studies local and regional ecosystems and presents human beings as a dominant animal. By contrast, Earth systems science conceives of the Earth as a total system and presents human beings as capable of influencing and disrupting that whole.[23] This point was captured and expanded upon by Will Steffen (2004: 1):

> the Earth itself is a single system, of which the biosphere is an active, essential component ... Second, human activities are not so pervasive and profound in the consequences that they affect the Earth at a global scale in complex, interactive and accelerating ways; humans now have the capacity to alter the Earth system in ways that threaten the very processes and components, both biotic and abiotic, upon which humans depend.

For Steffen, the Earth system is a unified, complex and evolving system. Its study is necessarily transdisciplinary and encompasses the "earth sciences and life sciences, as well as the 'industrial metabolism' of humankind, all within a systems way of thinking, with a special focus on the non-linear dynamics of a system" (Hamilton 2018: 12).[24] This is a novel perspective which explicitly supersedes the ecological worldview (Hamilton 2016). While the Earth is still positioned as an object, the intention is to study the entire system in a way that is dynamic and responsive to forces that range from the planet's core through to the atmosphere and beyond. The

Earth system is, in other words, a single and dynamic system rather than a collection of landscapes and ecosystems.

What might it mean to "rupture" this system? Hamilton's term is carefully chosen to illustrate that we are discussing something of much greater significance than a landscape impact. A rupture of the Earth system is a disruption of the functioning of the Earth as a dynamic totality. There are many ways to make this point, but Hamilton (2018: viii–ix) offers a vivid example that prompts us to think at the required scale:

> With knowledge of the cycles that govern Earth's rotation, including its tilt and wobble, paleo-climatologists are able to predict with reasonable certainty that the next ice age is due in 50,000 years' time. Yet because carbon dioxide persists in the atmosphere for millennia, global warming from human activity in the twentieth and twenty-first centuries is expected to suppress that ice age and quite possibly the following one, expected (other things being equal) in 130,000 years.

In other words, the rupture we are discussing is at the scale that the global climate has been irreversibly transformed for thousands of years. Human impacts have altered the course of planetary history (Matthews 2021: 6; Chakrabarty 2021). The question that motivates the present study is how law and governance might respond.

Method and Argument

The central argument of this book is that environmental lawyers need to engage the Anthropocene in a way that responds to Earth systems science, and which moves away from the idealism that pervades environmental legal scholarship. To pursue this argument, I engage in the method of critique. Critique, as Ben Golder (2021) notes, has a unique role to play in times of crisis because it can open ways of thinking that have been disguised by a certain curation of facts. My own approach is grounded in several diverse sources but is ultimately grounded in Ron Engel's notion of critical loyalty. This requires that interlocutors are read generously[25] and engagements are offered in "the spirit of self-reflective criticism" toward the "vocation we share" (2014: xv). Part of this is the refusal to equate critique with criticism (Heath 2012: 14) or the Critical Legal Studies (CLS) practice of trashing (Kelman 1984). As bell hooks (2010: 137) has argued: "[T]here is a useful distinction to be made between critique that seeks to expand consciousness and harsh criticism that attacks or trashes."

I situate critique as a systematic analysis of a theoretical formulation or a political problem that tries to bring to light premises and presuppositions that might not be readily available on the surface (Marx 1978a). Even if those foundations are wrong or misplaced, I contend that we can still learn something about what their wrongness systematises or represents. This generative aspect of critique is consistent with its etymology. As Wendy Brown notes, critique is derived from the Greek word κρίσις (*krisis*) which is a legal term for "sifting, sorting, judging and repairing" (Brown 2009: 9; Liddell and Scott, 394; Diggle 2021: 836). Critique then ought to have a restorative role in public discourse.

The substance of this book consists of four critiques of common arguments made by environmental legal scholars. For reference, those critiques concern the importance placed on anthropocentrism to explain the environmental impacts that have given rise to the Anthropocene; eco-constitutionalism; rights of nature; and ecological integrity. There is of course overlap between these arguments, i.e., anthropocentrism is a site of critique that unites most environmental legal scholars. Rights of nature can also be found in national constitutions. What unites my critique is that I regard each element as an example of philosophical idealism. More specifically, I will argue that there is something about legal scholarship that is focused on law reform that creates abstractions from the material conditions of daily life. I will also argue that the Anthropocene suggests a mode of analysis that is ordered around human beings and which engages directly with the material world.

In making this critique I draw on Marx's essay "On the Jewish Question" (1978a), which remains (in my view) the best critique of modern constitutional states. It is not necessary for me to summarise the essay here because Marx has engaged in specific debates and issues that do not concern us.[26] However, a brief statement will help elucidate a strand of the critique that unites the chapters that follow. Briefly, the part of Marx's essay that I am interested in is his engagement with the limits of political emancipation (what today we call equality before the law). To be clear, Marx thinks this is a positive step for those who have hitherto been legally discriminated against (1978a: 33). However, he also knows that political emancipation is not the same thing as full emancipation. It does not, for example, free people from those material forces that lead to inequality. Moreover, Marx argues that the State, by representing its subjects as free and equal, feigns an indifference to concrete forms of social power. Thus, even when we are politically emancipated, forms of social power still "act after their own fashion" (1978a: 33). They go from being categories that qualify a person for a position in the State to now just operating in civil society. They don't lose their power even as they cease to be a formal political force.

Another important aspect of Marx's essay that I draw on is his argument that when the State officially declares that a condition (property, race, gender etc.) does not matter to a person's political and legal status, it is also presupposing the existence of those powers. It is recognising their impact in daily life. Otherwise, the State would not seek to neutralise them through law. Drawing on this point, Brown (2002: 109) argues that the State is "premised upon that which it pretends to transcend" and gains a significant part of its authority through its claim to resolve inequalities which it entrenches and can only think about in a depoliticised way. Unfreedom and inequality are pushed into civil society where they are not named as political but are seen as the product of bad luck, the absence of hard work, or as natural. While Marx could not have foreseen it, there is an interesting link between this argument and the way neoliberalism, as a governing rationality, encourages people to personalise and individualise their response to the environmental crisis. I consider this aspect of the argument further in Chapter 2.

Drawing on this analysis I push Marx in a novel direction. To suggest that the most important task of the State is to enact formal equality and produce a level playing field upon which we can all compete is not a neutral position. To be indifferent to the powers that organise society – powers of wealth, education, race, gender, class etc. – is to side with the status quo. Neutrality sounds prejudice free. But if gender, for example, is a site of social power and something that limits a person's access to certain opportunities, experiences and institutions, then for the State to insist on blindness is to side with privilege. This kind of argument is ready made to apply to the Anthropocene. For example, if industrial capitalism and extractive industries are a major cause of the great acceleration, then for the State to feign neutrality is to side with capital.

This line of analysis will be both overt and implicit in my approach to critique. In engaging idealism, I also want to make clear that I do not deny the relevance of ideas (this is a book after all) to law and politics. During my analysis I will sometimes suggest a new way of looking at an old idea or suggest a concept that I think better responds to Earth systems science. My overriding concern will be to make sure environmental legal scholarship does not take a deterministic approach and suggest that ideas determine reality. While rarely[27] overt, I argue that this logic is implicit in legal scholarship that is focused on law reform. As a counter to idealism, I will conclude this book by sketching out what I think a materialist approach to environmental legal scholarship might take. Materialism, I argue, not only overcomes the limits of idealism but is also suited to an age that is ordered around human power. That is the calling card of the Anthropocene.

Notes

1 There is a distinction between environmental law and ecological law. See Anker et al. (2021) and Garver (2021). The distinction is not important for my argument but I will use the term "ecological law" when engaging scholars who specifically identify with this field.

2 I also acknowledge that environmental law has influenced the development of ecology through a process of testing and study. See Brooks et al. (2002). Ecology is a noteworthy omission from Coyle and Morrow (2004).

3 This is what Aldo Leopold (1993) called the "round river."

4 See further Monbiot (2014).

5 Precursors to this idea include the concept of "mutual aid" developed by Kropotkin (2021).

6 For a contemporary example of this slippage see Hollo (2022).

7 Donald Fleming (1972: 18) described Leopold as "the Moses of the New Conservation impulse of the 1960s and 1970s, who handed down the Tablets of the Law but did not live to enter the promised land."

8 Susan Fader (1979: 143) argued that Leopold wrote "in a strikingly different manner" not as an ethicist but as an ecologist.

9 Natural law thinking also opens a series of additional problems. See Shapiro (2011: 49–50).

10 See Burdon (2010) and Burdon and Williams 2016.

11 I have previously argued against seeing rights of nature as necessarily connected to Earth Jurisprudence. See Burdon (2014).

12 For a detailed commentary of misrepresentations see Hamilton (2018: 13–27).

13 As Jeremy Davies (2016: 70) has argued, the term Anthropocene "condenses into a single word a gripping and intuitive story about human influences on the planet." See further Kunkel (2017).

14 For an example of this thinking in the social sciences see Bonneuil and Fressoz (2017: 170, 198).

15 This slippage is most notable in Matthew's critique of Jeremy Davies. See Matthews (2021: 27).

16 Against this reading, Matthews (2022: 29) draws our attention to the fact that one of Paul Crutzen's early papers argued directly against a unified anthropos. See further Crutzen (2002).

17 See further Matthews (2022: 33).

18 Hamilton's (2018: 29) contention that debate about the term reflects the "semiotic turn" in the social sciences is his least convincing argument on this point. For stronger arguments see Matthews (2021: 33) and Angus (2016: 230–232).

19 For a summary see Angus (2016: 27–106).

20 Hamilton (2015b: 105) coined the term "golden-spike fetishism" to denote a preoccupation with debates on the start date of the Anthropocene.

21 The Anthropocene Working Group have selected "the mid-20th century" as the starting point because it "coincides with the clearest and most distinctive array of anthropogenic signals imprinted upon recently deposited strata." See further (Zalasiewicza et al. 2017: 58).

22 I follow Latour (2017: 87) in distinguishing Earth systems science from the Gaia hypothesis.

23 See Hamilton's (2018: 16–17) critique of Smith and Zeder (2013) and Ellis (2013) on this point.

24 See further Lawton (2001) who notes that Earth systems science studies "not only the processes that go on within each component (traditionally the realms of oceanography, atmospheric physics, and ecology, to name but three), but also interactions between these components." As Lawton notes, it is the *interactions* between these components that are central to the work of Earth systems science.

25 As I interpret Engel, he invites generous reading and a philosophical engagement that is constructive, mutual and directed toward a shared undertaking. It regards scholarship as a collective striving for knowledge and eschews individualism, competition or point scoring. See further Rawls (2000: xvii).

26 I have engaged the essay at length in Burdon (2021).

27 I say rarely because, as we will see in Chapter 4, some advocacy for rights of nature is couched explicitly in the language of an idea whose time has come.

Chapter 2

A New Anthropocentrism[1]

Anthropocentrism

A dominant strand in environmental legal scholarship argues that the dominant cause of the environmental crisis lies in the way Western culture conceives of the relationship between human beings and nature. More specifically, the argument is that human beings view themselves as separate from and superior to the environment (Bosselmann 1995; Capra and Mattei 2018). For writers like Lyn White Junior, this "anthropocentric" perspective had its deepest roots in Christianity and God's granting of dominion to human beings (1967: 1203). Others trace it back further to the ancient Greeks (Jensen 2005: 5) or to other critical points in Western culture such as the scientific revolution (Merchant 1990). Whatever the origin point, many environmental theorists contend that anthropocentrism needs to be replaced by an ecological perspective that views human beings as one equal part of a comprehensive Earth community (Garver 2021; Bosselmann 2017). In this context, human law may be considered subservient to the laws of nature or to the common good of the ecological community (Burdon 2014). Drawing on Hans Kelsen, others have argued that the integrity of ecosystems ought to be understood as a *Grundnorm* or basic norm upon which the authority of law is grounded (Bosselmann 2014).

In contrast to this scholarship, and as part of a revision of my own work, this chapter argues that a focus on anthropocentrism is insufficient for responding to the Anthropocene. This is for two reasons. First, the way anthropocentrism is constructed in environmental scholarship does not respond to those forces that make human beings unique and capable of causing a rupture in the Earth system. Clive Hamilton (2018: 43) is provocative on this point, arguing: "The problem is not that humans are anthropocentric, but that we are not anthropocentric enough … . we refuse to face up to the profound importance of humans, ontologically

DOI: 10.4324/9781003413370-2

and now practically, to the Earth and its future." For reasons explored in this chapter, I do not entirely subscribe to this view. But I think Hamilton is pointing in the right direction by asking us to confront the precise nature of the human condition in the Anthropocene. Second, I contend that a deterministic theorisation of anthropocentrism reflects the kind of philosophic idealism noted in the introduction.[2] From this perspective, scholarship that positions a mental conception of the world as the root of the problem and at the vanguard of social change fails to encounter the material forces at work in the Anthropocene. As I argue in the conclusion to this book, social changes occur through a dialectic of transformations across a range of moments and develop unevenly in space and time to produce all manner of local contingencies.

While I am critical of scholarship that takes a deterministic position on anthropocentrism, I don't deny its relevance for environmental thinking. I want to take the idea seriously and bring some nuance to the discussion. Thus, in the first part of this chapter I argue that anthropocentrism needs to be broken down into its component parts – perceptual, descriptive and normative. I argue that perceptual anthropocentrism is a necessary part of how humans engage with the world and that the Anthropocene has rendered descriptive anthropocentrism a scientific fact. What other conclusion could one draw from the idea that human beings have caused a rupture in the Earth system? However, against Hamilton's (2018: 43) assertion that human power requires us to be more anthropocentric, I argue that normative anthropocentrism is still something that needs to be challenged. Thus, I do not accept that we should affirm anthropocentrism as a valid description for the human condition in the Anthropocene.

If an engagement with normative anthropocentrism is to have meaning today I contend that it needs to engage material changes and dominant logics that have been developed during the Anthropocene period. Following my dating of the Anthropocene in the introduction, this leads me to focus on the idea of neoliberalism, which was cultivated by a transatlantic network from the 1950s onwards. While the term neoliberalism has been subject to many diverse interpretations, I am interested in exploring it as a governing rationality or dominant logic that plays a role in shaping our thoughts and patterns of thinking. Neoliberalism, I contend, contains normative anthropocentrism as an unquestioned assumption but it is also much broader and seeks to economise every aspect of daily life.

On my interpretation, the roots of neoliberalism can be traced to the writing of Jeremy Bentham whose utilitarianism and behaviourism promoted a unique form of human exceptionalism. Building on this work I describe how neoliberalism has become a dominant logic and how its precepts have framed advocacy within the environment movement itself. This presents a novel problem for those responding to the Anthropocene – because neoliberalism shapes our subjectivity, it cannot simply be discarded in favour of a different worldview. In fact, contemporary subjects may be unfree in a unique way in terms of our capacity to value the environment and Earth system on their own terms.

Unpacking Anthropocentrism

For many environmental legal thinkers, anthropocentrism is something that is objectively incorrect and unequivocally harmful. George Sessions (1974: 73), whose writing on deep ecology inspired some of the more idealistic strands of environmental law,[3] described anthropocentrism as a mode of thinking that separated human beings from nature and regarded the latter as existing for the use and exploitation of the human community. An example of this can be noted in property law which regards land as a commodity that can be traded or developed in an individualistic way and without regard for the ecosystem within which it sits (Freyfogle 2003). The same is true for non-human animals, many of which have been commodified, turned into property and often exist exclusively for human consumption or use (Francione 1995).

This is a common reading of anthropocentrism. And yet its simplicity ought to alert us to the possibility that something more complex is lurking. In this vein, Ben Mylius (2018: 159) argues that anthropocentrism be broken down into three separate ideas:

1. *Perceptual* anthropocentrism: which characterizes paradigms informed by sense-data from human sensory organs;
2. *Descriptive* anthropocentrism: which characterizes paradigms that begin from, center upon, or are ordered around *Homo sapiens*/"the human"; and
3. Normative anthropocentrism: which characterizes paradigms that constrain inquiry in a way that somehow privileges Homo sapiens/"the human" [passive normative anthropocentrism]; and which characterizes paradigms that make assumptions or assertions about the superiority of Homo sapiens, its capacities, the primacy of its values, its position in the universe, and/or make prescriptions based on these assertions and assumptions [active normative anthropocentrism].

This is a helpful intervention and allows us to describe environmental law as being concerned primarily with normative anthropocentrism – the contention that human beings alone have moral value and that our needs and desires ought to be privileged over non-human animals or the environment. While logical positivists (Ayer 2001) sought to remove human subjectivity from philosophy, I regard perceptual anthropocentrism as an inescapable part of the human condition. This alternative line of analysis can be found in writers such as Friedrich Nietzsche who argued that subjectivity is integral to the way we encounter and interpret the world. For example, in the context of a broader declamation about objectivity, Nietzsche (1989: 119) wrote:

> There is only a perspective seeing, only a perspective "knowing"; and the more affects we allow to speak about one thing, the more eyes, different eyes, we can use to observe one thing, the more complete will our "concept" of this thing, our "objectivity," be. But to eliminate the will altogether, to suspend each and every affect, supposing we were capable of this—what would that mean but to castrate the intellect?

As Nietzsche notes, seeing and knowing always takes place from an embodied and situated existence. There is no such thing as a purely objective presentation of a social fact, phenomenon, concept or a practice. We always see the world from an angle or through a lens, even if that is not immediately perceptible to us. With this in mind, I contend that we ought to affirm perceptual anthropocentrism as a necessary part of the human condition. Try as we might, we cannot "think like a mountain" (Seed 2007) and attempts in that direction risk anthropomorphising or falsely extending human consciousness onto the environment.

What about descriptive anthropocentrism? For most of human history this idea would have been nonsensical. For centuries, the natural world has been thought of as an immense and inexhaustible system. Annie Proulx (2016: 69) captures this sense in a novel depicting the 300-year deforestation of the Americas: "The forest was unimaginably vast and it replaced itself ... the profits could come forever." This sentiment can also be noted in law in the latter part of the 20th century. For example, the 1972 *Ocean Dumping Convention* was built on the assumption that the Ocean had an "infinite ability to assimilate waste" (Harrison 2017). More broadly, frameworks built around sustainability often include the idea of "stationarity" (Benson and Craig 2017), or the ability of natural systems to regenerate (Telesetky et al. 2019). Such assumptions are not legible in the Anthropocene where, as discussed in the introduction, we have observed a rupture in the Earth system as a whole. In fact, I contend that Earth systems science has rendered descriptive anthropocentrism an objective fact. Moreover, whether we accept it or not, the concept of the Anthropocene is premised on a worldview that is ordered around human beings.[4]

I return to this ordering in Chapter 3 but for now let us push this idea further to suggest that human beings are a unique and particularly powerful kind of animal. I don't see any reason to deny this and in contrast to Hamilton (2018: 28)[5] I contend that this is orthodoxy in mainstream scholarship. A recent expression of this point was made by Melanie Challenger (2021: 6):

> Opening our eyes, we face the truth of what we are, a thinking and feeling colony of energy and matter wrapped in precious flesh that prickles when it's cold or in love. We are creatures of organics substance and electricity that can be eaten, injured and dissipated back into the enigmatic physics of the universe. The truth is that being human is being animal.

And yet, as Challenger notes (2021: 21),[6] there is a world of difference between claiming that humans are animals and arguing that humans are *just* animals. The Anthropocene only underscores this fact by placing the future of the Earth system in the hands of a conscious force. Whatever valid critiques one might make against the centrality of human beings, the idea of the Anthropocene "arrives to blow them all away and instantiates humankind … at the centre of the Earth" (Hamilton 2018: 41). This places a peculiar burden on environmental legal thought. In particular, it requires that we disentangle the various meanings of and come to terms with descriptive anthropocentrism so that we can grapple with its normative implications. It is very difficult to do this if "anthropocentrism" is meekly accepted as an unequivocal negative that must be avoided at all costs.

Let us return now to normative anthropocentrism which has been the primary concern of environmental law. Drawing on the discussion of Hume's law in the introduction we should first note that there is nothing in the concept of the Anthropocene or Earth systems science that supports the normative elevation of human beings over the rest of the Earth system. Despite this fact, one can still find statements of human exceptionalism in response to the Anthropocene. It is rare to find this articulated as an explicit statement on the exclusive moral value of human beings. More commonly, it takes the form of an unquestioned assumption that the environment exists for human use (Washington et al. 2021) and that the Anthropocene presents an opportunity to complete human mastery over nature.[7] Ellis (2012) captures the point: "Most of all, we must not see the Anthropocene as a crisis, but as the beginning of a new geological epoch ripe with human-directed opportunity" (Ellis 2012).

This perspective is richly captured in the Ecomodernist Manifesto (2015). I don't want to exaggerate the importance of this document but, given the number of prominent scientists that have signed on to its contents, it is worth a brief engagement. The intention of the Manifesto is to create an audience[8] and position itself as a rallying point for those who are "optimistic" about our capacity to develop technologies that can regulate the Earth system. The tone is set right at the beginning: "we write with the conviction that knowledge and technology, applied with wisdom, might allow for a good, or even great, Ecomodernist Manifesto" (2015: 6). Here the words "great Anthropocene" should be read as indicating our capacity to bring the Earth system back under control and concomitant notions of human flourishing. In fact, an explicit goal of the Manifesto is to promote flourishing within the majority world.

To achieve this, the Manifesto argues that we need to explicitly reject the idea that "human societies must harmonize with nature to avoid economic and ecological collapse" (2015: 6). Given the range and extent of damage done to the Earth system, the authors contend that such harmonisation is no longer an option. Instead, the authors unconsciously adopt Francis Fukuyama's (1989) famous "end of history" thesis to argue that human societies have moved from "autocratic government toward liberal democracy characterized by the rule of law and increased freedom" (2015: 8). This evolutionary perspective of human societies has been roundly rejected – including by Fukuyama (2019) himself – but it provides stability for a series of policy proposals. The Manifesto calls for the intensification of activities such as agriculture, "decoupling humankind's material needs from nature," setting aside wild nature for protection, and a massive investment in technology (2015: 27, 28). While I think Hamilton (2018: 24) unfairly describes the Manifesto as a modern version of Francis Bacon's treatise on nature,[9] I do agree that it misrepresents fundamental aspects of Earth systems science and exaggerates the capacity of the environment to recover from human activities.[10] Ellis (2012) for example makes the surprising claim that "there is little evidence to date that [the dynamic between humans and nature] has been fundamentally altered." Reading Ellis generously we might interpret him as making a claim about the continued productivity of nature. A more expansive reading is difficult to sustain and cuts against the definition of the Anthropocene outlined in the introduction.

Suffice to say, there is no logical reason why affirming perceptual and descriptive anthropocentrism needs to result in an arrogant and hubristic approach to the Anthropocene. Nor must it promote the modernist myth of human exceptionalism. There is nothing incompatible with putting descriptive anthropocentrism at the centre of environmental law and proceeding with humility, uncertainty and caution. We inhabit a field of open texture and it is for us to decide how to fill it.

As we take tentative steps forward I contend that it is first important to recognise that the Anthropocene is not something that is open to refusal. Our collective future will be determined as much by the Earth system as by our own choices. As Isabella Stengers (2015: 47) notes, we will have to "go on answering for what we are undertaking in the face of an implacable being who is deaf to our justifications." We must take ownership over our new-found power and concomitant responsibility. It is far too late to try and step back, refuse responsibility and hope that the Earth system will return to some imagined "natural" state. This is a central tenet of Wilderness ethics (Nash 2014), which has had a profound influence on environmental law and notions of ecological integrity, discussed in Chapter 3. But it is ultimately a Holocene concept and unintelligible in the face of a rupture to the Earth system as a whole. Hamilton (2018: 54) expands on this central point:

> We can no longer withdraw and expect nature to return to any kind of "natural" state. There is no going back to the Holocene. We may have acquired it foolishly, but we now have a responsibility for the Earth as a whole and pretending otherwise is itself irresponsible. So, the question is not whether human beings stand at the center of the world, but what kind of human being stands at the center of the world, and what is the nature of that world

So what kind of human now stands at the centre of the world? Hamilton's question is impossibly ambitious. But even on a tentative approach I contend that a focus on normative anthropocentrism, as articulated in environmental law, is not sufficiently textured to help us navigate the Anthropocene. This is because most descriptions of normative anthropocentrism focus on a set of ideas that were developed during the rise of Christianity and the scientific revolution and treat them as sufficient for understanding the human condition today. This is an idealistic perspective in so far as it privileges ideas over material factors in historical development.[11] But even on its own terms it does not account for the emergence of new ideas that have occurred under industrial capitalism or how the self has been shaped in response to the logic of capitalism.

If normative anthropocentrism is to have value in environmental thinking today, it needs to engage with the kind of human that has been shaped since the advent of the Anthropocene. In particular, I contend that it needs to say something about how the logic of neoliberalism has shaped a unique kind of human – one that is unfree in novel ways. This does not purport to be a complete picture or even affirm that such a project is possible. However, given the connection between extractive capitalism and the Anthropocene (Malm 2015; Moor 2015), understanding this relationship will help us think politically about how to respond to the Anthropocene and shine some light on those structures of power that get in the way of an effective response. Moreover, engaging the logic of neoliberalism provides an opportunity to test my proposal in the introduction that the concept of the Anthropocene needs to be robust enough to hold not only its scientific understanding but also important points of critique.

Homo Oeconomicus

In the previous section I argued that scholarship in environmental law focuses on normative anthropocentrism and the claim that humans alone have moral value. This perspective also suggests that human beings are separate from the environment and that the natural world exists for human use and exploitation. While I agree with environmental law scholars that normative anthropocentrism is still something that needs to be confronted, I part ways in thinking that the version of history promoted within the literature is sufficient for diagnosing the present crisis. This is not only because it is idealistic but also because it essentialises a limited number of historical moments to explain the impact of a worldview on structures of law and governance. In particular, many expositions stop at the scientific revolution (Cullinan; 2011 and Capra and Mattei 2018)[12] and do not think about how normative anthropocentrism has developed since the industrial revolution or with reference to neoliberal capitalism. This analysis carries (at least) two implicit assumptions: first, that anthropocentrism is a determinate concept with identifiable boundaries; second that we can know all that we need about anthropocentrism by looking historically.

Against these assumptions, I suggest that normative anthropocentrism is an indeterminate concept which continues to evolve and take new forms. Its boundaries are less fixed than fuzzy and it will also take new forms in response to dominant ideas, social relations, changes in technology and material conditions. It may also be that engagement with other ideas and material conditions has not so much transformed normative anthropocentrism as generated a new idea entirely. It is not necessary for my argument to resolve this question except to say that I perceive enough similarity between normative anthropocentrism and the logic of neoliberalism to proceed with some caution.

In order to fully appreciate the logic of neoliberalism I contend that one needs to start not with the Mont Pelerin Society but with Jeremy Bentham.[13] One could go back further to Adam Smith and his figure of a merchant who pursued self-interest through processes of trade and exchange. But for my purpose, I am interested in the way Jeremy Bentham promoted human exceptionalism through a series of cost/benefit calculations. As we will see, Bentham had no strong commitment to specific values such as liberty or individual freedom and it is this absence that makes him particularly relevant to understanding the logic of neoliberalism and the ways it has influenced normative anthropocentrism today.

Bentham's Self-interested Subject

Neoliberal political philosophy brands itself as a new and updated version of liberalism. This is useful from a rhetorical perspective and allows neoliberal thinkers to claim heritage back to an intellectual cannon that includes Adam Smith and John Stuart Mill. For example, the legal scholar Henry Simons (1941: 213) positioned "the great political philosophers of modern democracy" as key conversation partners in his advocacy of free markets. According to Daniel Stedman Jones (2012: 12, 18), proponents of neoliberalism have promoted a particular history of liberalism that accentuated points of perceived connection. The end result was an à la carte approach to history which often failed to engage with the specific values of writers or their complex relationship with ideas such as utilitarianism.[14] If neoliberalism has any connection to this history, I contend that it is not through the liberalism of Mill but the utilitarianism of Jeremy Bentham.

One of Bentham's most important contributions to legal thinking concerns the way he called into question the increasingly popular idea that law and governance should be designed in a way to maximise individual freedom. This is an important moment in the history of normative anthropocentrism because it sharpened the focus from human good (understood as centring on wealthy, heterosexual, white men) to the individual. In some respects, Bentham is best read as writing against the grain of this moment. This is most clear in his attempts to marshal the logic of utilitarianism to advocate for the extension of rights to non-human animals. In an oft quoted passage, we can see Bentham's influence on the contemporary animal rights movement: "The question is not, Can they reason? nor Can they talk?, but Can they suffer?" (1948: 311). Bentham's utilitarianism necessarily also requires him to look beyond the rights and freedoms of individuals and toward the broader conception of general happiness.

Moreover, unlike the nascent liberal concerns with individual legal rights, Bentham is interested in exploring technologies of governance that could be put in the service of moulding and shaping behaviour. Implicit in his corpus is the idea that human beings can be coerced or manipulated toward "proper conduct" (Bentham 1969: 96). Most famously, his writing on the Panopticon is directed toward figuring out how to use basic human psychology to manipulate and control populations without having to use overt power or force (Bentham 2010). Thus, unlike liberal thinkers like Mill, Bentham is not wedded to values such as liberty and equality. These things might contribute to overall happiness but they are not sacred values. Neither were rights (Bentham 2002) or democratic ideals related to public participation (Schofield 2006). So, Bentham is not a liberal in the standard meaning of that term and he gives us a very different take on anthropocentrism from what we have encountered so far. Bentham probably affirmed human superiority over the environment and non-human animals (he was not a vegetarian after all[15]). But the key point is there are no values or principles that Bentham holds absolutely – other than the principle of utility. Everything is up for grabs, so long as it can be used to promote overall happiness (Bentham 1969: 85–86).

This is the key fact that makes Bentham's work so relevant for comprehending neoliberalism. While I think neoliberalism does have some core moral commitments,[16] it has demonstrated an incredible willingness to jettison values in the service of its deeper objective – the economisation of daily life. And by putting utilitarianism at the heart of his political philosophy Bentham set loose the creature that has been birthed by capitalism – the self-interested subject (Bentham 1969: 96). While often overlooked, this is a key moment for those advocating for recognition of the Capitalocene, coming as it does at the same moment that "Capitalists in a small corner of the Western world invested in steam, laying the foundation of the fossil economy" (Malm 2015: 64). While a utilitarian calculus could have been put in service of environmental protection, in practice, the environment was still cloaked in the vision of abundance noted above and regarded as a "cheap" commodity. As Jason Moore (2015: 62–63) contends, Capital "must ceaselessly search for, and find ways to produce, Cheap Natures: a rising stream of low-cost food, labor-power, energy, and raw materials to the factory gates (or office doors, or …)." For advocates of the Capitalocene, these so-called commodities are fundamental to the law of value in the capitalist mode of production (Moore 2015: 63). In fact, the ecological project of capitalism is to increase the amount of "unpaid natures"[17] in the total value of commodities that are produced for sale.

Another reason why Bentham's utilitarian calculus was not put in the service of conservation was because of the lingering influence of cartesian dualism noted by environmental law scholars (Bosselmann 1995; Harvey 1996: 123–124; Matthews 2021: 29). Advocates of the Capitalocene frame this in slightly different terms but the essential meaning is the same. Capitalism depended on a mode of thinking that separated humans from the environment or externalised nature from the costs of production. From this perspective, human agency is enacted on an inert object or commodity which cannot experience pleasure or feel pain. It is thus immaterial (in itself) from a utilitarian perspective. Moore (2015: 189) is explicit on this point, arguing that a new "law of value" was set in motion during the formation of capitalism:

> One was the proliferation of knowledges and symbolic regimes that constructed nature as external, space as flat and geometrical, and time as linear (the field of abstract social nature). The other was a new configuration of exploitation (within commodification) and appropriation (outside commodification but in servitude to it).

Here we can see how capitalism depends on a logic that separates humans from the environment. As Moore (2015: 31) notes: "Nature goes into one box; Society goes into another." Capitalism is thus haunted[18] by cartesian dualism and that logic is affirmed rather than challenged by the unique expression of human exceptionalism promoted by Bentham.

The final point about Bentham that is relevant to understanding neo-liberalism as a political rationality concerns his approach to governance. As noted above, Bentham is trying to develop technologies whereby people could be controlled without recourse to overt force. To achieve this, he looked to programmes of manipulation and control to get people to engage in what he considered proper conduct. Bentham (2002: 321) is explicit about this:

The greatest enemies of public peace are the selfish and the hostile passions: necessary as they are, the one to the very existence of each individual, the other to his security … Society is held together only by the sacrifice that men can be *induced* to make of the gratifications they demand: to obtain these sacrifices is the great difficulty, the great task of government.

This has an important implication for Bentham's utility principle when scaled up from the individual to political governance. Here it is easier to spot Bentham's biases against the desires of the masses and the measures he puts in place to prevent the utility principle being used to promote hedonism (Bentham 1969: 96–97). Rather than passively accepting the will of the demos, Bentham thinks that political leaders must play an active role in shaping desires.[19] And this can only be done by making the cost of gratifying antisocial desires very painful (Bentham 1969: 98). Bentham's theory of governance seeks to raise the principle of utility to the collective and find inducements that coerce people to behave in the "right" way (Bentham 1969: 97).

This is the genius of Bentham's work. He grasps that inducements to good behaviour do not lie simply in legal rules or systems or rewards/punishments. Rather, getting us to be proper subjects in a mass society is achieved through an organisation of space, and systems of discipline that penetrate to the very depths of the human beings and remake us and our desires. In other words, Bentham's politics seeks to shape us at the very core of our subjectivity. And, as explored in the next section, neoliberalism advanced this project much further than Bentham could have imagined.

The Neoliberal Subject

The term neoliberalism has been subject to many different interpretations. Compounding this is the fact that the term is often used imprecisely and is subject to contestation and denunciation.[20] Elizabeth Humphrys (2018: 53) has noted that different authors have used the term to refer to: "(1) a doctrine, set of ideas and/or ideology; (2) a set of economic policies, an entire economic regime and/or a distinct phase of capitalism; (3) a political project, form of political rule and/or type of state; (4) a category of denunciation or criticism; (5) a governing rationality; and (6) a complex mix of some or all of these elements." My own use of the term corresponds with the fifth option presented by Humphreys but as we will see the lines dividing these interpretations are blurry and there will be moments of cross-pollination. It should also be noted that this is not the dominant interpretation of neoliberalism which treats the term as a political project of the new right to impose privatisation and deregulation as a means for promoting negative liberty.[21]

Wendy Brown (2015: 17) has given the fullest expression of neoliberalism as a governing rationality, describing it as a "peculiar form of reasons that configures all aspects of existence in economic terms."[22] In describing neoliberalism as a "form of reason," Brown is talking about the way dominant ideas (or logics) in society influence not only the way we think but the kinds of ideas that are "thinkable."[23] This is easiest to grasp if we return to anthropocentrism and think about the ways ideas surrounding human exceptionalism took on a veneer of naturalness and inevitability. When a logic is dominant it is simultaneously an unspoken assumption and not something that needs to be defended. Something similar is true today from within the logic of neoliberalism. Notions of human exceptionalism are affirmed through an unspoken assumption that the environment exists as "cheap nature" and something to be valued through its productivity. If the environment cannot be economised, it does not have value. In the language of property law – it is waste.

A second key idea in Brown's description of neoliberalism as a governing logic concerns the economisation and the metrication of daily life. The process of economisation is widespread and encompasses activities that occur both within and outside of the economy. For example, Brown (2015: 31) writes: "we may (and neoliberalism interpellates us as subjects who do) think and act like contemporary market subjects where monetary wealth generation is not the immediate issue, for example, in approaching one's education, health, fitness, family life or neighborhood." Even the most intimate and personal parts of oneself can be coerced into this logic. For example, Brown (2015: 31) notes: "one might approach one's dating life in the mode of an entrepreneur or investor … [m]any upscale online dating companies define their clientele and offerings in these terms, identifying the importance of maximizing return on investment of affect, not only time and money."

Like the behaviourism promoted by Bentham, neoliberal rationality does not rely on force or overt power.[24] Its effectiveness lies in the way we are conscripted into self-discipline and model our own thoughts and behaviour after the model of the firm. Thus, Brown (2015: 33) argues that the project of neoliberalism "is to self-invest in ways that enhance its value or to attract investors through constant attention to its actual or figurative credit rating, and to do this across every sphere of existence." This is an apt description of the hustle economy and the wealth generation capacity of YouTube celebrities and social media influencers. But as Brown suggests, the reach of neoliberal rationality goes beyond these new economic actors. Even older professionals, such as university academics, are encouraged to comport themselves to the model of the firm by becoming an entrepreneur of their research, competing for research money, networking at conferences and advertising their research to the private sector.

Neoliberal rationality has perfected the techniques of self-discipline first envisioned in Bentham's Panopticon. It would also *seem* to be morally neutral – what matters is the economisation of daily life. Brown (2006: 692) has advanced this reading, arguing that neoliberalism is "expressly amoral at the level of both ends and means." However, just as we saw with Bentham's attempt at amorality in applying utilitarianism, this claim does not hold when we scale neoliberalism up as a tool for governance. Brown (2019: 11) has acknowledged this in more recent work that considers how a network of academics, business people, activists and journalists promoted neoliberalism in the transatlantic world.[25] According to Brown (2019: 11), this "neoliberal international"[26] sought to demonise "social and democratic" ideas of governance and replace them with "markets and morals."

Brown is not the only scholar to make this point. In an earlier study, Melinda Cooper (2019) provided a stunning inquiry into the ways patriarchal family norms have become embedded in welfare and educational reforms. She argues, for example, that efforts to privatise healthcare, social security and education involved shifting responsibility from the state to the individual in the provision of basic services. While not discussed by Cooper, something similar can be noted in the way individual responsibility is cast as critical to preventing environmental degradation and climate change (Sparrow 2021). In similar terms, Jessica Whyte (2019: 8) has presented the most detailed account of the moral foundations of neoliberalism. For Whyte, what "distinguished the neoliberals of the twentieth century from their nineteenth-century precursors [was not] a narrow understanding of the human as *homo oeconomicus*, but the belief that a functioning competitive market required an adequate moral and legal foundation." The key protection described by Whyte is human rights which were positioned as a tool for protecting the market and the private sphere (family and church) from social democratic movements.

I return to critique rights in Chapter four but for now two things need to be underlined: the first concerns how neoliberal governmentality stands in opposition to any kind of deliberative, democratic or state–administered social policy. The second is that while the logic of neoliberalism is orientated toward the economisation of daily life, it is not amoral but comes "dripping from head to foot, from every pore" (Marx 1992: 834)" with reactive values and assumptions of human exceptionalism.

The fact that neoliberalism is not purely instrumental is what opens it up to an engagement with normative anthropocentrism. But for environmental law scholars to take this step it will need to make several concessions. The first and most important is that normative anthropocentrism is not the sole or most important explanation for the environmental crisis. It cannot be presented as the ultimate root cause of the conditions that gave rise to the Anthropocene. Instead, normative anthropocentrism sits alongside other values which are not necessarily articulated or defended but take the form of an unspoken assumption. As noted above, there is no need to articulate an idea once it occupies the space of a dominant logic. Like the air we breathe it is everywhere and has the appearance of inevitability or naturalness. Second, rather than expressing itself as a worldview which can readily be supplemented by an alternative way of seeing the world, normative anthropocentrism is part of a governing logic which is part of subject formation. It is thus a much deeper part of ourselves and much more difficult to dislodge. With those concessions in place let us take a look now at how the logic of neoliberalism might help us think through environmental issues in the Anthropocene.

Neoliberalism and Normative Anthropocentrism

In the previous section I argued that normative anthropocentrism is an implicit assumption and starting position that neoliberal rationality takes for granted. Under neoliberalism, normative claims about the supremacy of human beings are not challenged. Nor is the idea that the environment exists as human property for use and exploitation. Because neoliberal rationality plays a role in subject formation it is actually harder for people to see the environment as an entity with its own unique value or agency. This is because the idea of nature having value is not something that can be economised. We thus have to work a lot harder to think in value-rich terms and often in relative isolation from the dominant logic in society. For these reasons we may regard contemporary subjects as unfree in a novel way – the idea of nature having value and agency is occluded by the more insistent imperative for economisation.

One of the most insidious aspects of neoliberalism as a governing rationality is it coerces us to participate in our own subjugation. The process of economisation operates at the level of our thoughts and language. It is thus possible for us to refer to the environment in terms of natural resources or natural capital. A functioning ecosystem is described in terms of ecosystem services. The depth to which this language has penetrated our society can be witnessed most clearly within the environmental movement itself. If one were looking for a collective of people versed and supported in thinking outside the logic of neoliberalism this might appear a reasonable place to start. However, as Hamilton (2011) has observed, the largest NGOs have come to rely on the "techniques of lobbying and media management that industry groups have perfected" and are increasingly staffed by "people with lobbying and media skills, and the conservative political outlook that goes with it."[27]

Because large organisations play an "agenda setting"[28] function this has a broader impact on how environmental issues are framed and presented to the public. To take one example: in Australia, campaigners for the protection of the Great Barrier Reef don't frame their demands in the language of intrinsic value or the importance of the ecosystem for marine life. The imperative of economisation incentivises them to think and talk in terms of tourism or the economic impact a dead reef will have on the Queensland economy (Smee 2018). Thus, the World Wild Life Fund (WWF) calls on the public to "remind our governments that it's their job to protect the Reef and the 69,000 jobs it provides" and Greenpeace states "reef generates over $6 billion for Australian's economy and supports 64,000 jobs, mainly through tourism."[29] These may be valid concerns but they are not the only or even the most important things that will be lost if the reef collapses entirely.

More pervasive is the attempt to place a dollar value on the functions the environment provides to sustain life. For example, the WWF noted that the environment underpinning all economic activity was presently valued at US$125 trillion (Fleming 2018a). In similar terms, a United Nations Environment Program called The Economics of Ecosystems and Diversity (2019) found that "an annual investment of $45 billion to biodiversity conservation worldwide could safeguard about $5 trillion in ecosystem services – a benefit to cost ratio of 100 to 1" (Fleming 2018b). The same logic can be noted in reports protecting natural capital. For example, a report from the International Monetary Fund (IMF) found that a single whale can sequester 33 tonnes of carbon dioxide over the course of its life. However, rather than advocating reserves or strengthening protections against hunting, the report argues that the whales should be commodified at a price of USD$2 million. Once priced, the whales can then be traded in a market to compensate countries and businesses that "incur significant costs as a result of whale protection." The report concludes that the IMF "is well placed to help governments integrate the macroeconomic benefit that whales provide in mitigating climate change, as well as the cost of measures to protect the whales, into their macro-fiscal frameworks" (Chami et al. 2019).

Far from isolated, this framing has become the dominant language of global environmental NGOs including the International Union for the Conservation of Nature.[30] Advocates of this approach are not wrong in holding that economisation provides a common language with the business community and a means for valuing the environment. However, economisation also contains the same shortcomings we encountered when discussing Bentham's utilitarianism. Namely, the principle of protecting the environment is not one that is held absolutely. It is always contingent and balanced against economic opportunity. Thus, if an environmentally significant project is valued at a greater price than the natural capital it is not clear on what grounds the venture may be opposed. Economisation crowds out other languages for expressing a justice claim and renders advocates for environmental protection vulnerable on their own logic. Finally, neoliberal rationality presumes that human nature is motivated exclusively by the profit motive and perpetuates a logic that presumes that "markets are more natural than nature itself" (Sparrow 2021: 185).

A similar problem can be noted in public policy initiatives for transitioning toward renewable energy. Barack Obama presented a master class on the logic of economisation during his 2013 State of the Union Address. Part way through his speech, Obama made an impassioned commitment to do more to tackle climate change. In the name of future generations, Obama implored the American people to "choose to believe in the overwhelming judgment of science – and act before it's too late" (2013). However, in the very next sentence, Obama shifted gears and argued that combating climate change is not only reconcilable with economic growth but necessary for achieving it. Here is the text:

> the good news is we can make meaningful progress on this issue while driving strong economic growth. I urge this Congress to get together, pursue a bipartisan, market-based solution to climate change … in the meantime, the natural gas boom has led to cleaner power and greater energy independence. We need to encourage that. And that's why my administration will keep cutting red tape and speeding up new oil and gas permits.
>
> (Obama 2013)

As Brown (2015: 25) has noted, Obama economises environmental concerns into matters for market, growth opportunities and as part of a broader agenda of national competitiveness. His reasoning begs a question – if economic growth and national competitiveness required America to double down on extracting fossil fuels would that be the right course of action? Reading Obama generously we might presume that this was not his intention. But again, we can see here how the logic of economisation displaces other values and justifications for transitioning to renewable energy. And while Obama does not need to explicitly advocate normative anthropocentrism, his indifference is not prejudice free. To be indifferent to the powers that organise society – powers of human exceptionalism and economisation – is to side with the status quo.[31]

Conclusion

This chapter has presented several intersecting arguments. It began with a critique of how environmental law scholars have engaged anthropocentrism and presented it as the root cause of the environmental crisis. Against this reading, I argued that perspectival anthropocentrism is a necessary feature of the human condition and that the Anthropocene has rendered descriptive anthropocentrism a scientific fact. Focusing then on normative anthropocentrism, I argued that a deterministic focus on a mental conception of the world is idealistic and fails to engage with the material causes of the Anthropocene. Even on its own terms, I also argued that environmental law scholars have neglected to think about how this idea has developed since the industrial revolution and, in key moments that most Earth systems scientists argue, date the beginning of the Anthropocene. If normative anthropocentrism is to have any explanatory power today, I argued that it must be brought into conversation with new ideas and modes of material production that speak to the human condition today.

With this ground work established, I focused my analysis on neoliberalism which I presented as a governing rationality or dominant logic. I argued that neoliberalism takes normative anthropocentrism as an unquestioned assumption and deepens notions of human exceptionalism by cultivating a form of subjectivity that seeks nothing less than the economisation of daily life. After presenting this as a political theory and noting its lineage in the writing of Jeremy Bentham, I also provided examples of how the logic of economisation has pervaded environmental discourse and campaigns. It must be stressed that this logic is much more complex than the idea of normative anthropocentrism presented by environmental law scholars. It is also more pervasive in that it shapes our subjectivity and recruits us into perpetuating the logic through language and ways of thinking. In fact, one of my contentions in this chapter is that those of us living under the logic of neoliberal rationality may be unfree in a new way and may find it harder to consistently think and act in a value-rich way. If that is true, the prospects for human survival in the Anthropocene are dim indeed.

I think it is possible to read Brown (2015, 2019) and other theorists of neoliberalism such as Michel Feher (2018) as suggesting that the takeover of *homo oeconomicus* is complete. At the very least this is where they place emphasis and their work does not linger on the limitations of this logic. However, a close reading finds important caveats. Brown (2015: 21), for example, argues: "Alertness to neoliberalism's inconstancy and plasticity cautions against identifying its current iteration as its essential and global truth and against making the story I am telling a teleological one, a dark chapter in a steady march toward end times." She also argues that the demos must work to "counter this civilizational despair" if we are to have any hope of creating a "just, sustainable, and habitable future" (2015: 222).

What tools might fit this task? In the next two chapters I deepen my critique of environmental legal scholarship by focusing on advocacy based on eco-constitutionalism and rights of nature. Because my critique aims to be generative, I use my engagement with rights of nature to argue for the primacy of obligations. This focus, I contend, is more suitable to the kind of humility that needs to be cultivated in the Anthropocene and I also argue that it provides a mechanism for thinking outside the logic of neoliberalism.

Notes

1 Part of Chapter 2 was first published in "Ecological law in the Anthropocene" 11(1–2) (2020) *Transnational Legal Theory*: 33–46. Permission has been granted by Taylor and Francis Group (https://www.tandfonline.com/).

2 It is a common trope in environmental thinking to place an idea at the vanguard of change. Other examples include the nature dictates argument (Diamond 2005) or a focus on changes in lifestyle and consumption (Hawken 2007). For a fuller discussion of this point, see Harvey (2010: 189–212).

3 Consistent with the introduction, I mean idealistic in the philosophical sense, i.e. the notion that ideas determine reality. Against this assertion I note that Ben Boer (1984), arguably the most important proponent of environmental law in Australia, was influenced by the social ecologist Murray Bookchin. I have not detected this explicitly anti-capitalist influence on other foundational texts in environmental law.

4 The clue is in the prefix – ἄνθρωπος (anthropos) meaning "human."

5 Hamilton (2018: 21) argues that there is "something desperate about arguments that equate human beings with chimps, dolphins and dogs when on any measure the unbribable gulf between humans and the rest of creation is blindingly apparent." I have not seen human exceptionalism expressed in such terms and I note that Hamilton does not provide any references to support his perspective.

6 For Challenger (2021: 21), the key difference between humans and other animals is culture: "Culture's achievement is to store information outside the body."

7 This is particularly prevalent in certain circles within geoengineering (Hamilton 2013). But again, I don't think this represents the mainstream view. For an alternative see Brent (2023).

8 Here I am drawing on Robin's (2016) contention that manifestos are not written for an audience – they call a public into being.

9 Bacon, for example, notes "My only earthly wish is ... to stretch the deplorably narrow limits of man's dominion over the universe to their promised bounds ... putting [nature] on the rack and extracting her secrets ... storming her strongholds and castles" (Bacon quoted in Farrington 1949: 62).

10 On this second point see Michelle Marvier et al. (2012) who note: "Nature is so resilient that it can recover rapidly from even the most powerful human disturbances."

11 For an overview of historical materialism see Marx (1978b). I return to this perspective in the conclusion.

12 My own engagement stops at the Industrial revolution which I now view as too limited. See Burdon (2014).

13 While I have not used his analysis, I note that Laval (2017) has also perceived the connection between Bentham and neoliberalism. My thinking was sparked by Wendy Brown (2015: 32).

14 The most obvious example is the positioning of Adam Smith as a proponent of unregulated markets (Jones 2012: 18). But other thinkers like Mill were also adopted in a partial and selective way. Jones (2012: 12) for example notes that politicians liked his "liberalism" but not his "utilitarianism."

15 More concretely, Bentham (1948: 282–3n) deployed utilitarianism to argue that animals suffer less at the hands of the butcher than in the world: "death they suffer in our hands commonly is, and always may be, a speedier, and by that means a less painful one, than that which would await them in the inevitable course of nature."

16 This is most clearly articulated in Whyte (2019) and Cooper (2019). Wendy Brown (2019: 11) has also reassessed her previous statements on neoliberalism (2006, 2015) to argue that neoliberalism aims at releasing "markets and morals to govern and discipline individuals.

17 The phrase "unpaid natures" was coined by way of analogy to the amount of unpaid labour that goes into commodity production. This is important because as Moore (2015: 100) notes: "Circulating capital is the forgotten moment in Marx's model ... It consists of energy and raw materials used up during a production cycle."

18 I borrow this term from Matthews (2021: 29).

19 For a broader history see Chomsky (2013).

20 For an overview of this debate see Humphrys (2016).

21 Humphrys (2018: 54–62) provides a more detailed account of the dominant narrative.

22 As discussed below, Brown (2019: 10–11, 86, 102) has reconfigured this argument in more recent work.

23 Mark Fisher (2009: 2) is making a similar point with his concept of capitalist realism: "The widespread sense that not only is capitalism the only viable political and economic system, but also that it is not impossible even to imagine a coherent alternative to it." My use of neoliberal rationality also shares similarities with his term "business ontology" (2009: 17).

24 Although force and violence are often integral to the implementation of neoliberalism in countries. See Humphreys (2018: 58–59).

25 Philip Mirowski (2018) refers to this network as the "Neoliberal Thought Collective."

26 The term was originally used by Jones (2012: 42).

27 For a detailed account see Klein (2015: 252–302) and Dauvergne and Lebaron (2014).

28 The phrase is from Hermann and Chomsky (1988).

29 There are exceptions to this narrative, particularly by groups that focus on marine life such as the Marine Conservation Society. But the dominant framing is in the language of economic impact.

30 For a detailed analysis see Taylor, Brown and Burdon (2020).

31 For an elaboration on this argument see Burdon (2021).

Chapter 3

Eco-Constitutionalism

The Anthropocene has sparked the imagination of scholars and led to many novel proposals for development and reflection.[1] Given the reform orientated nature of legal scholarship it is perhaps not surprising that most of this work operates within the parameters of liberalism and prioritises the importance of legislation and governance structures. This is particularly true of doctrinal scholarship which can essentialise the role of law in isolation from other forms of power as expressed in the humanities and political economy. Law, from this perspective, sits at the vanguard and drives change at the level of the economy and informal sources of power that course through civil society. To take a simple example – legislation that protects the environment can alter corporate behaviour by restricting certain activities and give people a sense of the value or importance of nature.[2]

Perhaps the most emblematic example of this are proposals to alter national constitutions in response to the Anthropocene. Revealing their connection to ecology, this practice is also called eco-constitutionalism. Within the literature, the central contention is that constitutions, as the highest authority in national law, should have a role to play in environmental protection. Louis Kotzé (2017: 11), for example, has argued: "A constitutionalised global environmental law and governance order would arguably be better able to respond to the Anthropocene's unprecedented exigencies than a non-constitutionalised one." Evidence suggests that many lawmaking bodies around the world agree. Reflecting a growth in environmental consciousness, three quarters of countries now have ecological protections of some kind incorporated into their national constitution (Boyd 2012: 47). Tim Hayward (2005: 3/15) even suggests that there is virtually unanimous agreement "about the importance of making some form of provision for environmental protection at the constitutional level, even if in the form of a state duty or objective rather than necessarily as a fundamental individual right."

DOI: 10.4324/9781003413370-3

I am not so confident and my intention in this chapter is to subject eco-constitutionalism to the method of critique described in the introduction. Rather than trashing proposals for eco-constitutionalism, I am interested in bringing to the surface its presumptions and asking why it has emerged as a popular response to the Anthropocene. My overarching argument is that eco-constitutionalism is an idealist discourse and promotes abstract representations of relationship between human beings and the environment. This, I contend, is critical to understanding why countries with ecological constitutions are unable to fulfil their commitment to environmental protection. Exacerbating this idealism is the fact that in many countries, the reform is presented from the top down and without a social base that can form an interpretative community for meaning making and enforcement. Finally, while eco-constitutionalism aims to be politically neutral, its silence on forces such as extractive capitalism, leaves untouched the most important powers that course through civil society and law. Purporting to be neutral to these powers is not value free and reinforces the status quo.

Eco-Constitutionalism

Many constitutions are silent on matters of environmental concern. Their focus is anthropocentric in the sense that they presume that only human rights[3] and powers are relevant for governance. By contrast, the phrase eco-constitutionalism tries to situate human action within a broader living system and to limit freedom for the good of the whole. Broadly speaking, the term eco-constitutionalism brings together two substantive areas of research: (1) the worldwide "greening" of national constitutions that has occurred since the 1980s and (2) the growing interest in "global constitutionalism" which seeks to identify and justify constitutionalist principles in international law. The most public example of the latter is the United Nations backed initiative to adopt a Global Pact for the Environment.

The idea of eco-constitutionalism precedes discussion of the Anthropocene. One important origin point is the German constitutional debates that were held between 1985 and 1990. Klaus Bosselmann (2017: 154–157) has done the most work to bring the substance of these debates to an English-speaking audience. He notes that during the 1980s the environmental movement had such a strong social base that it was able to instigate a public debate about the merits of a new state objective (*Staatsziele*). State objectives have a more formal standing than a policy position and Bosselmann (2017: 154) describes them as "binding constitutional law requiring government to seek to fulfil certain task." The constitutional debates were an exemplary form of public discourse and involved sophisticated discussions about whether the environment should be recognised as having intrinsic value or value because of the services it provided to human beings. In the end, a compromise was reached and Article 20a was incorporated into the basic law of Germany. The Article reads: "The State, also in its responsibility for future generations, protects the natural foundations of life in the framework of the constitutional order, by legislation, and, according to law and justice, through the executive and the courts" (Bosselmann 2017: 154).[4] Following further advocacy, an additional amendment was made in 2002 to include reference to non-human animals.[5]

While Germany was undergoing these changes, a similar push from civil society resulted in a different kind of amendment in the Swedish constitution. In 1992, Article 120 of the Federal Constitution was inserted to recognise the *Würde der Kreatur* or the "dignity of creation." The context for this phrase is an article regulating, and in some instances prohibiting, the use of gene technology.[6] In this instance, the phrase "dignity" does not quite capture the full meaning of the Article, as "dignity" has also been interpreted to mean that nature has its own core or essence (Bosselmann 2017: 155). This shares similarities to the idea of integrity discussed in Chapter 4.

While Germany and Switzerland led the "greening" of national constitutions they should also be located within a broader global trend in that direction. There are hundreds of examples which cannot be reproduced here. But to order this and provide a sense of the constitutional amendments that have been passed I have split examples into three groups: human rights, individual responsibility and obligations that are placed on the state (May and Daly 2014). For contrast and inclusivity, I have also selected examples from jurisdictions around the world and from majority/minority countries.[7]

Group 1: Constitutions that recognise a human right to a healthy environment:

> *Angola – Article 39(1): Everyone has the right to live in a healthy and unpolluted environment and the duty to defend and preserve it.*
>
> *Benin – Title II, Article 27: Every Person has the right to a healthy, satisfying and lasting environment, and has the duty to defend it.*
>
> *Cape Verde – Part II, Title III, Article 72(1): Everyone shall have the right to a healthy, ecological balanced environment, and the duty to defend and conserve it.*

Portugal – Part I, Section 3, Chapter 2, Article 66(i): Everyone has the right to a healthy and ecologically balanced human environment and the duty to defend it.

Group 2: Constitutions that place the onus of responsibility on the individual to protect the environment:

Czech Republic – Charter of Fundamental Rights and Freedoms, Article 35(3): In exercising his or her rights nobody may endanger or cause damage to the environment, natural resources, the wealth of natural species, and cultural monuments beyond limits set by law.

Finland – Chapter 2, Section 20: Nature and its biodiversity, the environment and the national heritage are the responsibility of everyone.

France – Charter of the Environment, Article 2: Everyone is obliged to take part in the preservation and improvement of the environment. Article 3: Everyone shall, subject to the conditions defined by the law, avoid any disturbance which he or she is likely to cause to the environment or, if that is not possible, limit its consequences. Article 4: Everyone shall contribute to the reparation of the damages which he or she caused to the environment, subject to the conditions defined by the law.

Group 3: Constitutions that place obligations on the state to protect the environment:

Columbia: It is the duty of the State to protect the diversity and integrity of the environment, to conserve the areas of special ecological importance, and to foster the education for the achievement. The state must also cooperate with other nations in the protection of the ecosystems in border areas.

Sudan – Chapter 11(1): The State and the citizens have the duty to preserve and promote the country's biodiversity.

Yemen – Article 35: Environmental protection is the collective responsibility of the state and the community at large. Each individual shall have a religious and national duty to protect the environment.

This is just a very brief overview and of course many countries combine these approaches or place legal duties on citizens to protect the environment. For example, Chapter 2, Section 6, Article 86 of the Constitution of Poland holds: "Everyone is obliged to care for the quality of the environment and shall be held responsible for causing its degradation." In a similar way Chapter 2, Article 58 of the Constitution of the Russian Federation holds: "Everyone is obliged to preserve nature and the environment and care for natural wealth." And finally, Article 71 of the Constitution of Ecuador is even more ecocentric, holding that nature itself has the right to "integral respect for its existence and for the maintenance and regeneration of its life cycles, structure, functions and evolutionary processes."[8] Linked to these rights is a broad standing provision that empowers all "persons, communities, peoples and nations" to "call upon public authorities to enforce the rights of nature." And finally, Article 72 places obligations on the Ecuadorian state to restore despoiled nature, including in circumstances where the damage was caused by the "exploitation of non-renewable natural resources."

In fact, the greening of national constitutions has occurred concomitantly with a burgeoning academic literature, the overwhelming thrust of which is that constitutional law can and should play a key role in environmental protection. For example, David Boyd (2012: 3) argues: "While no nation has yet achieved the holy grail of ecological sustainability ... evidence ... indicates that constitutional protection of the environment can be a powerful and potentially transformative step toward that elusive goal." In agreement, Klaus Bosselmann (2017: 231) argues: "the proposed grounding of the rule of law in nature by implementing an environmental grundnorm appears to be an appropriate way forward." While more hedged in his advocacy, Louis Kotzé (2016: 11) presents a similar argument:

> constitutionalism should also be a vital component of the global regulatory arsenal that is currently being shaped as a social-institutional response to the Anthropocene's socio-ecological crisis ... a constitutionalised global environmental law and governance order would arguably be better able to respond to the Anthropocene's unprecedented exigencies than a non-constitutionalised one.

It is hard to disagree absolutely with these statements. Even if their intentions are not fully realised, I would prefer to live in a world where environmental protection is an express goal in the highest legal and political document in a country. If nothing else, it provides advocates with a language to articulate environmental concerns and call out double standards or hypocrisy. While totally insufficient it is not nothing. In saying this I should also be clear that no advocate for eco-constitutionalism has suggested that it is a sufficient reform in the absence of other changes at the level of culture or the economy. While not expressly noted by the authors above, some of this hesitancy can be noted in their language. For example, Bosselmann's term "appears" and Kotzé's phrase "arguably better" contain humility and imply limits on relying on a constitutional response to the Anthropocene. With that in mind I turn now to consider critiques of eco-constitutionalism.

Eco-Constitutionalism as Idealism

There is a burgeoning field of critical scholarship on constitutionalism and concomitant notions of sovereignty. One important intervention comes from Daniel Matthews (2021: 7) who engages sovereignty as a "framing device and a mode of perception" that does not adequately respond to the Anthropocene. Matthews notes that sovereignty is usually constructed in a bounded way – at the level of a population, territory or national state (2021: 159). However, in a situation where human impacts have a planetary significance, there is a clear sense in which our political and legal forms are radically insufficient. Matthews argues further that sovereignty, as an expression of human social organisation, deliberately excludes the environment from its purview. The Earth system, from this perspective, is the backdrop upon which the human drama is played out and agency is expressed. For Matthews it is this peculiarly modernist view that needs to be challenged and reframed with the recognition that we are Earthbound.

While affirming this critique my own engagement rests on a distinction between two philosophical schools – idealism and materialism. A perfect line cannot be drawn between these two schools of thought and in practice they influence one another. An idealist, for example, will emphasise the role of ideas in determining material reality and driving historic change. When faced with a problem, such as the environmental crisis, an idealist will emphasise the importance of adopting an alternative worldview (such as ecocentrism) or focus on strategies grounded in public education. In legal scholarship, an idealist will focus attention on law reform that either constrains choice or promotes certain kinds of behaviour or ways of seeing the world.

Materialism, by contrast, is an alternative philosophy which holds that what moves history is the organisation of material life or how human societies subsist and reproduce themselves. The most reduced way we might speak about this today is the political economy of the economic order of human existence (Marx 1978b). Because materialism is not a dominant framework today, its insights may be less intuitive for readers. The easiest way to understand this is to reflect on how changes in the material order – from feudalism to capitalism for example – solidified a particular version of the family form, modes of social organisation and social relations. It has been argued, for example, that class structures and patriarchal norms can be traced to the capitalist mode of production (Farrelly 2011). Thus, from a materialist perspective, the environment crisis is not primarily the result of anthropocentrism or other dominant ideas. It is the result of how we organise the means of production in a capitalist economy (Harvey 1996). I return to flesh out his perspective in the final chapter of this book.

With this background in place, I contend that eco-constitutionalism reflects and perpetuates a form of philosophical idealism. Following my understanding of critique outlined in the introduction, I do not present this as an unequivocal negative. Rather, I contend that a critical engagement provides an opportunity to enquire why eco-constitutionalism has risen to prominence at his time and what its politics presumes that is not accessible from the orthodox description. My conversation partner in this analysis is Karl Marx who was the first to draw out this line of critique and think about the limits of an idealist approach to history. His 1848 essay, "On the Jewish Question" (OJQ)[9] circles around the question: what is it about constitutional states that limits their capacity to deliver on their promises to deliver freedom and equality for all citizens? Central to Marx's critique is his contention that constitutional democracies emerge from the nature of capitalist production. With the emergence of constitutional democracy, Marx argued that citizens concentrated on how things are described in law rather than focusing on how they are experienced in material life. Put otherwise, there is a growing split between the idea of freedom and how that is experienced by flesh and blood individuals.

In making this statement Marx is not suggesting that constitutionalising ideas such as freedom and equality is a bad idea. In fact, the opposite is true. Marx (1978b: 35) was explicit that constitutional states are an improvement on feudalism and other systems of legalised inequality. He argues further that enshrining freedom in the constitution is the "the final form of emancipation within the framework of the prevailing social order." In other words, it is the best outcome under a liberal constitutional state. However, Marx is noting that, as the focus of politics turned to the conditions of formal equality (what Marx called political emancipation) and how individuals were described in law, the gap between our political and material life grew. This was not the case under feudalism where a person's legal status corresponded directly to their experience in daily life. Amongst other things this also meant that struggles for emancipation could be named as political rather than becoming entwined in the contention that formal equality had been achieved.

A version of this debate plays out in struggles for equality today. While undeniably an improvement on overtly discriminatory practices, laws directed at formal equality may not challenge the powers that course through civil society and limit certain kinds of access based on race, class, gender, sexuality etc. Thus, there is a gap between how a person is conceived in law and their daily life. In response, it may be stated that abstract legal representations are best understood as an ideal form toward which democratic politics must strive. This aspirational reading of political emancipation is entirely legible, but it is limited for those still labouring under forms of oppression, for whom it would be experienced as an abstraction.

This was as true for the Jewish community that Marx was engaging in with OJQ and it remains true for people today that march under the banner #BlackLivesMatter and #Metoo.

A key question for those advocating a form of eco-constitutionalism is how do you convert an abstract idea, i.e., humans have a right to a healthy environment into reality? And can you achieve environmental protection by placing constitutional reform at the vanguard of change? Marx did not think so. His contention in OJQ is that the split between abstract representations of human beings and the reality of our material difference is commensurate with an emphasis on idealism as a dominant form of political rationality. That is why, he argues, constitutional states are unable to deliver on their promise to guarantee equality or emancipation for all citizens. Change that is grounded in idealism might emancipate us politically but not at the deeper level of our material lives. Radical or deep change requires not only substantive legal reform *but* also a focus on materialism which for Marx means the ways we produce and reproduce our daily existence. At his stage of his career, Marx does not yet have a clear answer to the question about what full human emancipation might look like in practice.[10] But that is not the purpose of his critique, and he will, of course, provide an influential answer in subsequent writings, which I return to at the conclusion of this book.

Staying for now with Marx's critique, I contend that the same method of critique utilised in OJQ can be applied to eco-constitutionalism. While it might be an improvement for a national Constitution to contain a substantive statement about human rights to a healthy environment or impose obligations on the Government to guarantee clean air or water for citizens, we should also be attentive to how this kind of reform widens the gap between our political and material lives. This is particularly less eliminated than depoliticised through abstract legal statements. It is also possible that eco-constitutional reform will lead to no substantive change in environmental stewardship. This has been the case in countries like Ecuador which, after recognising the rights of nature in their constitution, have maintained an extractive economy that continues to threaten areas such as the Galapagos Islands. Moreover all the countries listed above with constitutional provisions related to the environment continue to despoil their environment and very few are taking steps to live within Earth's carrying capacity.[11] There are complex reasons for this and nobody is holding out eco-constitutionalism as the panacea for the environmental crisis. But if I was going to recommend eco-constitutionalism as a strategy for environmental protection, it would be useful to see some evidence of its effectiveness.

Following Marx's method in OJQ[12] we might also ask what is it about this historical moment that has given rise to eco-constitutionalism as a popular response to the Anthropocene? Here we should note that most advocacy is coming from scholars working in international environmental law.[13] Within this literature, the most common justification is the stakes of the environmental crisis and the evident failure of domestic and international politics to adequately respond. While not explicit, "crisis" is at the heart of most proposals and eco-constructionism is constructed as a political project aimed at leveraging the constitution for our protection. We are only talking about it because other avenues and strategies for environmental protection have not worked (or are not working). To paraphrase Robert Macfarlane (2019), eco-constitutionalism is part of our Anthropocene moment: "At once hopeful and desperate, it is a late-hour attempt to prevent a slow-motion ecocide."

In noting this I am not trying to suggest that emancipatory projects cannot emerge out of a crisis.[14] Only that we should be honest about the rationale for eco-constructionism and think about how its potential is marked by the circumstances of its inception. We might think, for example, about whether there are any risks associated with leveraging a governance document at a moment of political emergency. Progressives might be happy to do this for environmental protection, but there is a longer history of emergency politics being used for reactionary ends (Agamben 2005). It is also far from obvious that crisis provides fertile soil from which progressive reforms can emerge. Commenting on the 2019–2020 Australian bushfires, the economist Paul Krugman (2020) observed: "The sick irony of the current situation is that anti-environmentalism is getting more extreme precisely at the moment when the prospects for decisive action should be better than ever."

Increasing this risk is the fact that outside of academia there is no strong evidence that the demos support or are organising for a constitutional response to the Anthropocene. This is not uncommon for idealist approaches to law reform which invariably rely on the power of the idea to bring people along and drive history forward. This is captured in the oft-quoted phrase "an idea whose time has come"[15] and assumes that law can be at the vanguard of social change. What this approach misses are the material conditions for social change and the value of reform that is driven by a social base. If eco-constitutionalism was advanced as a response to the Anthropocene it would mean that citizens have not done the vital work of internalising the ideas, thinking about their meaning and understanding how their application would necessitate changes at the level of the economy. To borrow a simile from Joseph William Singer (2000: 3), the idealist approach to law reform assumes that a proposal can be handed down fully formed – like Athena emerging from the head of Zeus. In contrast, emancipatory proposals are something we collectively define and construct. They are like a piece of music that "unfolds over time" and "gets its sense of stability from the ongoing creation and resolution of various forms of tension" (Singer 2000: 3).[16]

Connected to this concern is the fact that the constitutional statements noted above do not directly confront what materialists consider to be the root causes of the environmental crisis. Eco-constitutionalism is a more abstract demand from laws that legislate binding targets to reduce emissions in line with the Paris Climate Agreement or place a moratorium on new fossil fuel extraction. A materialist perspective would also concentrate on the inconsistency between capitalism and environmental protection and advocate measures to transition the economy away from the capitalist mode of production (Harvey 1996; Moore 2015; Malm 2015; Saito 2017). Once change has occurred at the level of the economy, that is a flow on effect for technology, the relations between humans and nature, the reproduction of daily life, social relations and our mental conceptions of the world. There is, of course, a lot missing from this view but its intention is to focus on the conditions of our material reality and not abstract representations of ourselves.

A natural reply to this analysis would be to suggest that we do not need to choose between idealist reforms and material changes to the way our society reproduces itself. A variation of this reasoning suggests that reform at the level of the constitution can be the thing that drives substantive change at the level of economy and society. It is not my intention here to foreclose these possibilities or to suggest that there is only one right way to address the substantial environmental difficulties we face. We need people working at all levels and a healthy scepticism toward anybody that suggests that they have all the answers. However, it is my contention in this chapter that eco-constitutionalism only rises to the level of political emancipation and risks staying at the level of political emancipation without addressing the more systemic reasons for environmental destruction. Moreover, because we are operating on a limited time scale, it is also important to be strategic about where we place our emphasis.

One way that materialist and idealistic approaches to environmental protection differ is in the extent to which they name and expressly engage the powers that are giving rise to a problem. The constitutional provisions listed earlier in this chapter are phrased in neutral language and are largely apolitical.[17] This approach is useful if one is seeking to build a broad coalition of support and avoid conflict by naming a material structure such as capitalism. However, to be indifferent to the powers that organise society is ultimately not a neutral position – it is to side with the status quo. For example, if capitalism is a power that coerces corporations to find new markets and opportunities for extractivism, then for a constitution to feign neutrality or talk in general terms about environmental human rights, is to side with existing sites of power. It also forecloses other languages for expressing justice claims and leaves us with the instrumental language of *homo oeconomicus* described in Chapter 2.

Conclusion

My primary goal in this chapter has been to subject eco-constitutionalism to a constructive form of critique and bring to the surface the presumptions and presuppositions that underpin this approach to politics. Specifically, I argued that eco-constitutionalism contains an idealist vision of history which promotes change by presenting an abstract vision of human–earth relations. This creates a gap between how the environment is regarded at law and everyday processes of exploitation which are sanctioned by the same system. I also argued that eco-constitutionalism fails to engage many of the material causes of environmental exploitation, including causes at the level of the economy which are central to the eco-socialist critique of the Anthropocene. Neutrality about these factors maintains business as usual and may strengthen the status quo. With that in mind it is not surprising that there is no evidence that countries who have "greened" their national constitutions have stronger environmental records. In fact, an underlying argument in this chapter has been that eco-constitutionalism can only be idealistic if it is applied in the context of capitalism and extractive economies.

While they do not frame the debate in these terms, advocates of eco-constitutionalism are very much aware of the limits of their argument. That is why scholars such as Bosselmann and Kotzé pair their advocacy with other reforms that they contend are necessary for realising substantive visions of sustainability. I also agree with Bosselmann and Kotzé that campaigns for constitutionalising environmental protection are an improvement on systems of governance that are overtly exploitative.

They may also give civil society a language through which to point out hypocrisy and demand more radical forms of change. Where we differ, I think, is that I contend that emphasis should be placed on strategies that are driven from below and that have the potential to challenge the material causes of the environmental crisis. Without this emphasis, I fear that the only thing eco-constitutionalism will liberate is more coal. McKenzie Wark (2016: xiv) outlined this fear in the context of the Anthropocene:

> Of all the liberation movements of the eighteenth, nineteenth and twentieth centuries, one succeeded without limit. It did not liberate a nation, or a class, or a colony, or a gender, or a sexuality … What it freed was chemical, an element: carbon. A central theme of the Anthropocene was and remains the story of the Carbon Liberation Front.

While this analysis has focused on constitutional reform, my concern with idealist approaches to law carry over into the next chapter where I turn to consider the prevalence of "rights talk" in environmental discourse.

Notes

1 The best overviews are Kotze (2017) and Lim (2019a). See also Burdon and Martel (2023a).
2 The psychological aspect of law reform is less certain but can be noted in attitude surveys.
3 Countries like Australia have implied rather than express rights i.e. the implied right to political communication was recognised in *Australian Capital Television v Commonwealth* (ACTV) (1992) 177 CLR 106.
4 The German constitution also recognises that human property comes with inherent obligations. See for example, article 14 notes: "Ownership creates obligations. Its use shall at the same time serve the common good." Scholars have read this to include the good of the ecological community. See for example Raff (2003).
5 The section now reads: "Mindful also of its responsibility towards future generations, the state shall protect the natural foundations of life and animals by legislation and, in accordance with law and justice, by executive and judicial action, all within the framework of the constitutional order." See Basic Law

for the Federal Republic of Germany: https://www.btg-bestellservice.de/pdf
/80201000.pdf.

6   Article 120 reads: "(1) Persons and their environment shall be protected against
abuse of gene technology. (2) The Confederation shall legislate on the use of
the reproductive and genetic material of animals, plants, and other organisms.
In doing so, it shall take into account the dignity of creation and the security
of man, animal and environment, and shall protect the genetic multiplicity of
animal and vegetal species."

7   All of these translations are from May and Daly (2014).

8   For the full text see: http://pdba.georgetown.edu/Constitutions/Ecuador/eng-
lish08.html.

9   For a fuller analysis, Burdon (2021).

10 At this early point in his career Marx (1978b: 46) has not really figured out a
strong position on emancipation and only offers some brief thoughts which will
be developed in subsequent work. For example, he argues: "Human emancipation will only be complete when the real, individual man has absorbed into
himself the abstract citizen; when as an individual man, in his everyday life, in
his work, and in his relationships, he has become a *species-being*; and when he
has recognized and organized his own powers (forces propres) as *social* powers
so that he no longer separates this social power from himself as *political* power."

11 There are various ways of measuring this. See for example Erickson (2018).

12 A central idea for Marx in OJQ is that to ask a question properly is to begin to
resolve it. That is why his essay begins with a question "What kind of emancipation do they seek?" (1978b: 26). Scholars adopting my methodology might
adapt this approach for their own research. For example, it is always productive
to ask: What was it about this historical moment that has led to the x being presented in the way that it has? What are the contradictions in the existing political
and social and economic life that keeps us from being able to resolve x?

13 The examples noted above have emerged either because of the power of the
Green Movement (Bosselmann 2017: 154–157) or were included as part of a
broader process to modernise outdated governance instruments.

14 Although the historical record suggests that crisis is more often an opportunity
for even more predatory forms of capitalism and exploitation. See Klein (2008),
Lilly (2012) and Loewenstein (2017).

15 The phrase is attributed to Victor Hugo but can be noted in countless proposals
for law reform.

16 Singer is writing with respect to property law, but his reasoning applies to law
more generally.

17 Even the language of human rights seeks to be politically neutral and appeal to
universal ideals. See Moyn (2012).

Chapter 4

Rights and Obligations[1]

Since the 1970s legal rights have emerged as the dominant language for articulating all manner of justice claims. This is most notable in the proliferation of human rights instruments which emerged "seemingly from nowhere" (Moyn 2012: 3) and can be noted in many of the constitutional provisions extracted in the previous chapter. The dominance of rights-talk is so extensive that if one is looking for alternative concepts to ground a justice claim then the research tends to be historical.[2] Consistent with the exposition of neoliberal rationality in Chapter 2, I also contend that rights-talk has been subsumed within neoliberal rationality and thus appears as "the only game in town." Legal rights are particularly susceptible to the logic of neoliberalism because of their inception point in the individual and competitive notions of hierarchy.

In response to the dominance of rights, a critical scholarship has emerged (Golder 2017; Douzinas 2000). For the most part, this work has focused on social justice issues and substantive notions of human emancipation. Drawing on these lines of inquiry I am interested in exploring the relevance of the literature to the proliferation of rights in response to the environmental crisis and the Anthropocene. In one sense it is not surprising that rights-talk has proliferated in this space – as Wendy Brown (2004: 461) has argued, rights organise political space, "with the aim of monopolizing it." However, to date there has been insufficient critical engagement by proponents of environmental and ecological law. My intention in this chapter is to provide such a critique and suggest that there are compelling reasons for placing obligations at the centre of our response to the Anthropocene.

Rather than trying to provide an overview of rights instruments in this chapter, my specific focus will be on rights of nature. My intention here is not to pick an easy target for critique but instead to engage one of the most prominent sites of reform proposed by environmental law scholars. Consistent with previous chapters, my critical analysis is grounded in

DOI: 10.4324/9781003413370-4

trying to understand why rights of nature have emerged at this historical moment as a proposed solution to the Anthropocene. Against idealistic arguments that rights are *an idea whose time has come*, I will argue instead that rights of nature have emerged as a minimalist alternative that can be accommodated within the confines of industrial capitalism. Moreover, while advocates of rights of nature contend that legal rights are an indeterminate concept that can be filled with meaning, I argue that they are bounded to notions of individualism, competition and human good.

Rather than advocate rights, I join other scholars in advancing the priority of obligations. Like rights, obligations are also a contingent concept that carry baggage from the past. However, I argue that obligations are a better tool for a legal and ethical approach that is ordered around human beings. Rights enable us to externalise the problem and project concepts onto nature. But the problem is not "out there." The problem is with "us" and structures of capital accumulation that have given rise to the Anthropocene. Focusing our attention on obligations also goes some way to combating the risk that embracing aspects of anthropocentrism will lead to a hubristic or arrogant approach to the Anthropocene. My engagement with obligations draws on legal scholars such as Daniel Matthews and political theorists such as Simone Weil and Hans Jonas. Jonas in particular is important to my argument due to his understanding of the ways human power has been extended by technology and the risk this poses for the fate of the Earth.

The Turn to Rights

Advocates for rights of nature tend to ground their argument in ecological thinking and an expansion of human morality. The argument can be summarised as follows: human beings exist as one part of a mutually dependent ecosystem. If we have inherent value and the capacity for legal rights, then so does the rest of nature. This argument is most pronounced amongst advocates of Earth Jurisprudence and is grounded in Thomas Berry's (2006) document: "Ten Principles for Jurisprudence Revision."[3] It is not necessary for me to reproduce the entire list, but two key points are:

> The natural world on the planet Earth gets its rights from the same source that humans get their rights: from the universe that brought them into being.
>
> Every component of the Earth community, both living and non-living, has three rights: the right to be, the right to habitat or a place

to be, and the right to fulfill its role in the ever-renewing processes of the Earth community.

A theologian by training, it is not surprising that Berry adopts the logic of natural law in his advocacy for rights. This is most pronounced in his oft quoted statement: "the world is a communion of subjects, not a collection of objects" (2006: 17–18). While it is not clear if Berry is using the term "rights" in a moral or legal sense, it is certainly the case that many proponents of Earth Jurisprudence have positioned rights as central to their reform agenda.[4] However, this is not universally true, as some critics have claimed. Matthews (2021: 38), for example, has argued that rights of nature is a central tenet of Earth Jurisprudence and appears to suggest that scholars within that community have advanced rights in response to the Anthropocene. This critique does not properly engage with scholarship that positions Earth Jurisprudence as a theory of law and not a set of reform proposals. It also ignores writing that is sceptical or indeed hostile to the language of rights and the context within which such arguments are made (Burdon 2014; Burdon and Williams 2016).

If we look at the Anthropocene literature itself, it is far more common to find rights of nature arguments advanced from within what might broadly be described as liberal responses to the Anthropocene. This is not surprising given the centrality of individualism and rights to liberal political theory. María Valeria Berros (2019: 28) for example, argues that rights of nature are an "innovative and important proposal" which suggests a "growing democratization of environmental law." Seth Epstein (2022) has argued that rights of nature have been catalysed by indigenous political struggles for "self-determination and environmental activism." In agreement, Michelle Lim (2019b: 225) positions rights of nature as a method for incorporating "Indigenous worldviews into legal systems" and Carmen Gonzalez (2017: 232) argues that they represent a principle from "traditional legal systems that can be incorporated into contemporary environmental law." Finally, Saskia Vermeylen (2017: 139) has described rights of nature as a "counter force to the principle of commodification and capitalisation of nature" and Stefan Knauß (2018: 702) argues that they are foundational to stewardship ethics. This is just a very small sample of voices engaging rights of nature in direct response to the Anthropocene. Following my method in Chapter 2 I am interested now in thinking about why rights of nature have emerged at this historical moment in response to the Anthropocene.

While arguments for the rights of nature have their own distinct history (Nash 1989), I contend that the most important reason for their current prominence is the popularity of rights-talk in political discourse. Put another way – rights of nature have been swept up and carried in a broader political turn towards legal rights. This argument stands in contrast to the way rights of nature are portrayed in idealist jurisprudence as an "idea whose time has come"[5] or as a powerful tool for protecting the environment against the excesses of extractive capitalism (Boyd 2017). Against these framings, I argue that the ascension of rights is precisely because they are a minimalist alternative to the status quo. Further, while advocates of rights of nature have attempted to construct approaches that move away from human individualism, I contend that the discourse is constrained by its history and marked by its point of origin.

In thinking about a critique of rights, it is important to first note that they have always had detractors. The political right worry about giving discretion to the courts and expanding privileges beyond a defined class. While the left has stressed the ways rights configure us as isolated monads and fail to actualise substantive notions of emancipation. My own critique brings rights of nature into conversation with a branch of critical human rights scholarship. Central to this is Samuel Moyn's (2012) revisionist history of the ascendency of human rights. Contrary to the orthodox narrative which dates the proliferation of human rights instruments to the aftermath of the Second World War, Moyn argues that the term only gained traction from the 1970s. More controversially, Moyn argues that human rights instruments gained traction to counter more radical demands made by the anti-colonial movement and international communism. In this account, human rights rose to prominence because they did not require a commitment to sharing power, a redistribution of wealth or a radical restructuring of society. Human rights were fundamentally individualistic and could be accommodated within capitalism and even interpreted in a way that promoted the values of economic growth and individualism. Wendy Brown (2004: 461) has made a similar argument, noting that rights can come to stand as a "critique of dissonant political projects" and converge "neatly with the requisites of liberal imperialism and global free trade and legitimates both as well."

Alongside this literature, Jessica Whyte (2019: 6) argues that human rights became "the dominant ideology of a period marked by the demise of revolutionary utopias and socialist politics." Key for Whyte is the way theorists within the Mont Pelerin Society worked to position human rights as a protection for the market and private sphere (family and church) from social democratic movements.[6] As an example, Whyte cites the focus Amnesty International had on religious and political dissidence in the Soviet Bloc and the work of Médecins Sans Frontières and

Helsinki Watch (Human Rights Watch) to build connections with the neoconservative movement and the US State Department. For Whyte (2012), these human rights organisations offered not only a "moral gloss to neoconservative anti-communism" but, more fundamentally, a "stark warning against those emancipatory projects that sought to challenge the emerging economic orthodoxy of neoliberal capitalism." Reflecting on these examples, Whyte (2019:12) concludes that human rights are not only compatible with neoliberalism, but they were also actively promoted to encourage individuals towards self-interest, family responsibility and submission to "the impersonal results of the market process." In this way, human rights have become the "moral language of the competitive market" (Whyte 2019: 28).

While distinct, a similar kind of critique can be made of rights of nature. For example, in countries where rights of nature have been legislated, advocates have not been able to challenge any of the structural causes of environmental harm. This is perhaps most notable in Ecuador which, as mentioned in Chapter 2, has implemented rights of nature in their national constitution. Here it must be recalled that this constitutional reform was motivated, in part, by well-organised and indigenous-led movements in response to decades of environmental harm (Akchurin 2015). The demands of this movement have changed over the decades but there has always been a consistent thread of sovereignty and a concomitant greater level of decision-making authority over indigenous lands. Seen in this light, rights of nature are a retrograde step. The Constitution may contain some indigenous language (referring to nature as Pachamama for example) but unless an indigenous community has time, resources and expertise to bring a case in the Constitutional Court, the provision does not have the teeth to challenge oil extraction. This is supported by the fact that since 2008 there has not been a single case that has challenged oil extraction or led to greater compensation for communities impacted by pollution.

Those promoting the Capitalocene will point to more fundamental reasons why rights of nature legislation have (so far) proven to be ineffective. It is difficult to see how rights of nature can have real meaning in the context of extractive capitalism. In 2021 Ecuador's national oil corporation generated US$12 billion in revenue from oil – an increase of 22% from 2020 (Alves 2022). This accounts for a significant portion of Ecuador's GDP and the state-owned company has plans to double production over the next five years (Valencia 2022).[7] What substantive impact can rights of nature legislation have in the context of such extraction? Similarly, Bolivia has struggled to reconcile legislation for rights of nature with its desire to exploit the 5.4 million tonnes of lithium that sits below the Salar de Uyuni salt flat. Given the world's hunger for lithium to power the renewable revolution one wonders how long this part of the environment will remain protected.

Here we might note that advocates of rights of nature often draw an analogy between their movement and the granting of rights to slaves (Cullinan 2008).[8] The comparison is apt but not in the sense intended by advocates. Just as emancipated slaves remained in bondage and subject to the powers of racism that coursed through civil society (Downs 2015), the examples in Ecuador and Bolivia suggest that creating rights for nature may do nothing more than affirm a different form of subjugation. John Livingstone (1994: 173) has made this point, arguing that rights of nature arguments play "directly into the hands of zero-order humanism." Rights of nature is not a substantive or transformative alternative. They are not about displacing growth economics or democratising power in a way that empowers communities or builds resilience. Rather, a right of nature represents a minimalist alternative and seeks to mitigate environmental damage from within the co-ordinates of the current system. And, to date, it is proving radically ineffective.

This leads to my second point. Contemporary legal rights are fundamentally liberal rights, and they took shape adjacent to the birth of the individual (Siedentop 2017: 333) and the rise of legal positivism. Bentham (1987: 53) captured the latter point with his description of natural rights as "nonsense upon stilts." Increasingly, during the 18th century, rights were formalised in legislation and national constitutions to limit the role of government and protect the sphere of the individual (Siedentop 2017: 334). A lot has changed about the nature and function of legal rights, but this basic goal remains true today. Thus, for example, Ronald Dworkin (1978: xi) has argued that "[i]ndividuals have rights when, for some reason, a collective goal is not a sufficient justification for denying them what they wish, as individuals, to have or to do, or not a sufficient justification for imposing some loss or injury upon them." Similarly, Joseph Raz (1986: 250) contends that rights "mark matters which are of special concern" to the individual and are special for this reason.

There is a tension in applying a tool developed for the explicit purpose of protecting individual human interests to represent the interests of interconnected ecosystems or the Earth system. This tension is rarely acknowledged by advocates of rights of nature who instead regard rights as a tool that can be shaped to their purpose. Here we need to draw a distinction between arguments that rights are indeterminate (Kennedy

2002) and the suggestion that they are endlessly flexible and sufficiently suited for environmental protection. Susan Marks (2009: 1) helps us engage with this problem with her writing on "false contingency." She begins with her phonetic namesake, Karl Marx and his comment: "Men make their own history, but they do not make it just as they please in circumstances they choose for themselves; rather they make it in present circumstances, given and inherited" (1978c: 595; Marks 2009: 1). The problem, according to Marks (2009: 2), is that we tend to forget the second half of this statement and the ways in which the horizons for our future are bounded by the past:

> To be clear at the outset, I believe it is quite right to hammer the point that history is a social product, not given but made … [and that being made] it can be remade differently. This … cardinal principle of all progressive thought is as urgent as it is endless … . However, we may be undertaking this work in a way which causes us to neglect the equally important progressive point that possibilities are framed by circumstances. While current arrangements can be changed, change unfolds within a context that includes systematic constraints and pressures …. Things can be, and frequently are, contingent without being random, accidental or arbitrary.

For Marks, "false contingency" names the condition of thinking that things can be made anew or constructed from a blank slate. For our purpose, it means that lawmakers do not have boundless freedom to determine who or what is a rights holder and the content of those rights. This is not a question of human finitude but, as Ben Golder (2015: 87) reminds us, it is "a directly political question concerning the present limits to rethinking social and political arrangements—limits often embedded and iteratively reproduced within those very arrangements themselves." One way those limits are revealed is in the way that rights for nature have been shown to be conducive, not to environmental protection, but to a narrow conception of human flourishing. The "nature" instantiated within rights of nature discourse should also be understood not as exhaustive but as a "reflection of extant power relations" (Golder 2015: 87).

Thus, when New Zealand declares that the Wanganui river is a legal person with rights, those rights must be interpreted and enforced within existing power relations. While the interests of nature might make inroads at the margins,[9] there has not yet been a case where they have challenged economic interests in the river. Moreover, the definition of the legal person captured by the *Te Awa Tupua (Whanganui River Claims Settlement) Act* (2017) cannot exhaust the meaning of the river itself or the latent possibilities of interpretation that are practised by the local Maori Iwi.

Advocates of rights for nature omit to engage with the problem of "false contingency" and the material constraints that prevent certain ideas about nature as a rights holder from being realised. Or to express this point differently, while the idea of "nature" that emerges from rights of nature discourse is open to contestation and diverse interpretations, a "legal right" is a specific modality that shapes and limits the definitional possibilities of nature as a rights holder. Advocates of rights of nature cannot offer a blank slate because legal rights are bounded by the modality of rights and the historic meaning that people have brought to that term. This is true for any legal idea we seek to apply to the environment but "rights" appear particularly limited and susceptible to be arranged in a way that promotes economic growth over environmental protection.

The Centrality of Obligations

In Chapter 2 I argued that the Anthropocene provokes us to situate human beings at the centre of environmental ethics and law. It is insufficient to theorise the Anthropocene as merely describing extreme environmental harm or as another expression of ecological thinking. While the phrase "paradigm shift" is subject to overuse, I follow Hamilton (2018: 13) and Angus (2016: 27 & 32) in suggesting that it is an appropriate descriptor for thinking through the fundamental shift in thinking required by the Anthropocene. We have an opportunity to think about what a radical reorientation of environmental law may look like – one that is consistent with the human condition in the Anthropocene.

In social and political theory there is no such thing as a radical break from the past. We cannot invent a new language or set of descriptors that perfectly captures ethics in the Anthropocene. Neither can we look to nature for a syllogism that responds to Earth systems science. Our efforts will necessarily be connected to the old paradigm and contingent in the same sense as described in the previous section. But to accept these limitations does not affirm that all ideas are equal or contain the same potential for responding to the Anthropocene. With that in mind I turn now to think about the potential of obligations as a legal concept which is orientated around human beings, and which has the potential to displace the hegemony of rights.

To date, the foremost exponent of this shift is Daniel Matthews (2018, 2019, 2021). Matthews approaches obligations from a different angle to the present study. Rather than seeking an ethics that is centred around the human, Matthews is interested in the potential for obligations to open a "set of ontological concerns about the nature of our being-bound in place, in community and to a range of biotic and abiotic forces that exceed the human" (2021: 41). The phrase "bound to place" references Bruno Latour's (2017: 281) contention that the human beings are not living in harmony but "contending" with the Earth system.[10] From this perspective, we can no longer regard what Latour calls "Gaia" as a passive or inert object that is indifferent to our actions. Rather, human beings and the Earth system "share the same fragility, the same cruelty, the same uncertainty about their fate."

Living with this condition unsettles many long-held views about the place of human beings in nature, the meaning of interconnectedness and notions of harmony that pervade ecological legal writing. It forces us to confront the familiar with new eyes and to think differently about the enlightenment idea that human freedom is exercised on a passive object. This is what triggers Matthew's interest in obligations – if human beings are bound to the Earth system, we need to think differently about the bonds that constitute and limit social life (2021: 41). This puts the focus squarely on human beings and the obligations we owe one another. This is distinct from rights which externalise the problem – suggesting that the issue is "out there" and does not immediately require human beings to alter their behaviour. Because obligations are ordered around human activity, they also have the potential to limit the risk that accepting aspects of anthropocentrism will lead to a hubristic or arrogant normativity as discussed in Chapter 2.

Like rights, obligations also come with their own history and set of contingencies. It is, for example, difficult to talk about obligations without invoking Christian notions of imperative (Rawls 2000: 7). This presents a problem because outside of moral agreement or the threat of state violence, secular notions of obligation may have little political weight. I will return to this problem below, but it is noteworthy that in his advocacy of obligations Matthews draws on the political theory of Simone Weil. Weil is a useful conversation partner because she was also concerned with the proliferation of rights and the ways they reflect the uprootedness of modernity.[11] Moreover, while Weil's writings are scattered with Christian textual references, her writing *attempts* a secular theorisation of obligations in the style of political theology.

According to Weil (2005: 86), rights sit alongside democracy and notions of human personality in the "middle air" between "supernatural good and evil." Because of their adversarial nature and commitment to the personal, rights are something that "will inevitably do [people] harm" and "cannot root themselves in the Earth" (2005: 86). Weil presents these statements as an a priori conclusion which a reader is invited to accept/reject without defence.[12] Moreover, the illusion to "rootedness" ought not be read as invoking an ecological sensibility. Rather, rights are situated within Weil's dichotomy between the material and supernatural. More startling is Weil's next statement where she notes:

> It is the light falling continually from heaven which alone gives a tree the energy to send powerful roots deep into the earth. The tree is really rooted in the sky. It is only what comes from heaven that can make a real impress on the earth.
>
> (2005: 86)

Clearly, we have not moved too far from the Christian influence on obligations. Matthews does not engage this aspect of Weil's essay but only because it is not central to his reading. Instead, he focuses on Weil's contention that obligations "come before that of right which is relative and subordinate to it" (Matthews 2021: 42; Weil 2001: 2). In what sense are obligations prior? Weil's answer shares a similar logic to Wesley Newcomb Hohfeld's (1917) classic study on how the term "right" correlates with a duty. Specifically, she notes that a right is "not effectual by itself" and presumes the existence of an obligation "to which it corresponds" (Weil 2001: 2). Obligations, on this account are prior because they recognise and give effect to the right. That is sound reasoning, but one cannot read Hohfeld and not ask the next question – if obligations were prioritised in law would that not make rights prior in exactly the same sense? If not, what is it about obligations that enable them to "take root" away from the middle air?

One response to the question of priority comes from Weil's concern with shifting our focus from the personal to the impersonal. Weil uses the term "impersonal" to describe those *needs* which are most essential to the lives of human being and the obligations they entail. In the final years of her life, Weil listed some of these needs in her "Draft for a Statement of Human Obligations" (1943).[13] The list includes basic goods such as food, clothing, access to medicine and housing as well as the guarantee of safety from violence. These needs are imminent to the human condition and thus prior to their formalisation in positive law. Another way to put this is that obligations contain a deep ethical claim based on their necessity for human flourishing and communal life. Weil (1943) provides examples to help us understand the fine distinctions she is drawing between obligations and rights:

> If someone tries to browbeat a farmer to sell his eggs at a moderate price, the farmer can say: "I have the right to keep my eggs if I don't get a good enough price." But if a young girl is being forced into a brothel she will not talk about her rights. In such a situation, the word would sound ludicrously inadequate.
>
> (1943)

In this example, the farmer is making a personal claim: why do I have less than someone else? But the young girl is asking a different kind of question – why am I being hurt? This is an impersonal plea. For Weil, the language of rights is inadequate to redress this kind of harm because she links rights to property[14] and the girl has not been cheated of profit. She has been robbed of her humanity and there is no compensation for such a loss. Moreover, by focusing our attention on personal rights over impersonal demands, our attention is drawn away from what is really at stake. As Weil notes: "There is something sacred in every human being, but it is not their person. It is this human being; no more and no less" (1943).

As noted above, Weil was not writing in the context of the environment. But it is not difficult to apply her thinking for this purpose. Take for example one of the numerous proposals to expand coal mining in Australia. Environmental campaigners might respond that the government does not have the right to approval such a proposal or that the environment has a right to regenerate and flourish. But we can frame the same problem in the language of obligations – it is unjust for the government to grant licences for fossil fuel extraction because such an act will punish the physical and mental well-being of current and future generations. While the language of rights ignites what Weil called "the spirit of contention" the latter might "touch and awaken at its source the spirit of attention." The language of obligations is connected to empathy and the attempt to attend to the lives of others – including the non-human world. As Weil (2005: 224–225) notes:

> Anyone whose attention and love are really directed towards the reality outside the world recognizes at the same time that he is bound, both in public and private life, by the single and permanent obligation to remedy, according to his responsibilities and to the extent

of his power, all the privations of soul and body which are liable to destroy or damage the earthly life of any human being whatsoever.

This is an example of how obligations might root our thinking in place and community. Weil is describing obligations as part of the basic and reciprocal bonds that are necessary for collective living. This is fundamentally a moral point, but Weil argues further that it is a crime to refuse those obligations (2005: 225) and that any legal system that does not protect them "is without the essence of legality" (2005: 226). Matthews (2019: 12) does not address these aspects of her thinking, but he affirms that the privileging of obligations "offers a radically different 'legal screen' ... to that offered by rights, mediating social relations in a distinct configuration" (2019: 13). Matthews is interested in the potential for obligations to shift us away from regarding the state as sitting at the "heart of political life" (2021: 43). In this sense I regard his provocation as an important contribution to the "living law" (Ehrlich 1975: 17) that sustains communal relations and enriches social life.

However, rather than follow Matthews directly, I am interested in exploring how the Anthropocene can be interpreted as presenting a challenge to enlightenment notions of freedom and morality. While Kant considered freedom to be essential to morality and the human condition, such a pure dichotomy no longer holds (Hogue 2008: 191). As noted in the introduction, Earth systems science describes a human subject that is embedded in an earth system – not just a localised ecosystem. This subject has more power than ever before and our freedom is being exercised on a planet that is not passive, but increasingly hostile and unpredictable. This is an anti-humanist perspective in so far as it recognises that our future will be determined as much by the Earth system as by our own choices (Hamilton 2018: 54). Isabelle Stengers (2015: 47) describes the influence of the Earth system on our lives as a kind of intrusion:

> This is perhaps what is most difficult to conceptualize: no future can be foreseen in which she will give us back the liberty of ignoring her. It is not a matter of a "bad moment that will pass," followed by any kind of happy ending – in the shoddy sense of a "problem solved." We are no longer authorized to forget her. We will have to go on answering for what we are undertaking in the face of an implacable being who is death to our justifications.

We can push this point further to say that in the Anthropocene, the consequences of human agency are planetary. Contra Kant, morality is not rooted in freedom but in our embeddedness within the Earth system (Hamilton 2018: 52). The accompanying obligations to care for the Earth are much greater than traditionally expressed in ecological law and must be actively discharged. It is insufficient to project rights onto nature or engage in personal ethics as critiqued by Weil. Instead, human beings must come to terms with our new-found power and concomitant obligations. These elements – power and obligation – should be viewed as two sides of the same coin. And while this reading underlines human uniqueness, it does not celebrate it or view human beings as having exclusive moral standing. As Hamilton (2018: 54) explains: the Anthropocene "elevates human specialness in order to highlight our powers and their dangers, and so the obligations that go with them."

Before moving to this analysis, I note that an important thread of environmental writing has engaged with "post-humanist" and "new-materialist" studies. I part ways with Hamilton (2018: 91–98) and his critique of this work which he dismisses as part of the poststructuralist turn in environmental philosophy. What is most disappointing about Hamilton's engagement is that he does not provide a close or generous reading for writers such as Anna Tsing, whom he reads as "deflating human power and control," while inflating the "agency of non-human matter" (2018: 94). To my mind, Hamilton's misreading (whether deliberate or not) is attributable to his polemical style in *Defiant Earth* and also to his obvious impatience with anyone that does not ground their engagement with the Anthropocene in Earth systems science. However, there is also something gendered about this engagement with key feminist writers. Laura Rickards (2017) picked up on this as well, noting: "the masculine orientation of the book combined with his rapid dismissal of the arguments of key female voices on the Anthropocene, such as Donna Haraway, is unfortunate and limiting." It is not necessary for me to pursue this line of inquiry further since my aim is to think about ethics in a way that is centred around the human. But at this fork in the road, I note an alternative branch of scholarship which uses the Anthropocene context to focus attention on other agentic subjects within the Earth system (Matthews 2021; Davies 2022).[15]

In environmental scholarship there is a long tradition of thinking about obligations and responsibility.[16] Much of this also has a theological tone but draws more immediately from the influence of ecology described in the introduction. Thus, for example, Aldo Leopold (1949) reflected on notions of interconnectedness when articulating his land ethic.[17] Beyond this literature I am interested in thinkers who prioritised obligations, not because of ecology, but in response to the devastating power that human beings now possess. The richest source are thinkers (like Weil) who are writing in the aftermath of the Second World War and the dropping of nuclear weapons on Hiroshima and Nagasaki. This historical moment marks the dawn of the great acceleration and it inspired Hans Jonas to think carefully about the potential of responsibility as a necessary part of the human condition. His book, *The Imperative of Responsibility* places human beings at its centre and was one of the first texts to clearly articulate the need for human beings to take responsibility for the future of the biosphere (1979: 7, 136–137).

Jonas's appreciation for the vulnerability of life was etched into his consciousness during the Second World War. Here Jonas was a member of the Jewish Brigade of the British army and volunteered for combat duty. Commenting on this experience, Jonas (1980: xii) wrote:

> The apocalyptic state of things, the threatening collapse of a world, the climatic crisis of civilization, the proximity of death, the stark nakedness to which all the issues of life were stripped, all these were ground enough to take a new look at the very foundations for our being and to review the principles by which we guide our thinking on them.

Influenced by these experiences, Jonas sought to construct a theory of moral responsibility that was applicable to both the public and the private sphere. As noted, Jonas recognised that new technologies have given humanity power to cause enormous harm to other humans, to future generations and to the balance between humans and nature. In language that prefigures the Anthropocene, Jonas wrote:

> Modern technology, informed by an ever-deeper penetration of nature and propelled by the forces of market and politics, has enhanced human power beyond anything known or even dreamed of before. It is a power over matter, over life on earth, and over man himself; and it keeps growing at an accelerating pace.
>
> (1979: ix)

Jonas correctly identified that Kantian notions of freedom and morality provided an insufficient response to these circumstances. "All previous ethics," argued Jonas (1979: 1),

> had these interconnected tacit premises in common: that the human condition, determined by the nature of man and the nature of things,

was given once and for all; that the human good on that basis was readily determinable and that the range of human action and therefore responsibility was narrowly circumscribed.

By the 1970s the ground had already shifted out from under each of these ideas. Moreover, since ethics is about human action, Jonas argued that the "qualitatively novel nature of certain of our actions has opened up a whole new dimension of ethical relevance for which there is no precedent in the standards and canons of traditional ethics" (1979: 1).

Rather than advancing a theory of rights, Jonas focused on restricting human action. This is a challenging endeavour because Jonas felt that our glorification of science and technology had led to an ethical vacuum: "A nihilism in which the near-omnipotence is paired with near-emptiness, greatest capacity with knowing least for what ends to use it" (1979: 23). We are in a state of emergency, but without the tools to deliver ourselves from it. However, despite this, he argued that the "lengthened reach of our deeds" pushed obligations into the "center of the ethical stage."[18] Put another way, the "ought" or "obligation to do" or "restrain from doing" arises when we consciously exercise self-control: "In sum: that which binds (free) will and obligation together in the first place, power, is precisely that which today moves responsibility in[to] the centre of morality" (1980: 130). In addition to this, Jonas argued that the human capacity to take on obligations for others placed us in a unique position to care for and maintain the world for future generations. He called this the "ontological imperative" or "man's ought-to-be" (1996: 108).

At this juncture we are still left with a pressing question – if the nature of human power and our embeddedness within the Earth system provides a reason for responsibility, what is our motivation? Some writers claim that there is none. Hamilton (2018: 155–156), for example, argues that for all of its worthiness, "appeals to responsibility have no heft, no ontological substance." I have some sympathy with this conclusion – particularly as we have witnessed governments around the world fail to respond adequately to the environmental crisis. But it also feels like a conclusion drawn out from despair or as if ethical motivation requires a higher being to love or fear. Be that God or Gaia.

Clearly a new ethics cannot be conjured from thin air – it awaits realisation and articulation by humans fully inhabiting a new epoch. Moreover, it is important to underline that Jonas was at pains to describe his ethic of responsibility as an "option" (1996: 108). He was too shrewd a philosopher to contravene Hume's law or position obligations as a syllogistic response to human power. He was also cognisant of the possibility that we may fail to activate deep notions of responsibility. To activate ethics, Jonas argued that we need to engage human emotion and imagination. To this end, Jonas (1979: 85) wrote:

> For that enjoinder to reach and affect me, so that it can move the will, I must be receptive for appeals of this kind. Our emotional side must come into play. And it is indeed of the essence of our moral nature that the appeal, as insight transmits it, finds an answer in our feeling. It is the feeling of responsibility.

This perspective does not engage materialism or suggest that changes to the ways our society produces and reproduces itself can give rise to new ways of thinking. However, despite this limitation, I maintain that Jonas is articulating something important about the relationship between ethics and emotion. To borrow again from David Hume (1960: 415): "Reason is the slave of the passions in the sense that practical reason alone cannot give rise to moral motivation." In part, this is why I am interested in stories and fables that can tap into an emotional centre that logic and facts can miss (Burdon and Martel 2023b). We might thus regard Jonas's appeal to emotion as a partial and limited response for how an ethics of obligation can give rise to new forms of conduct that are grounded in thick notions of responsibility.

Conclusion

This chapter has provided a critique of rights of nature to understand why they have emerged as a prominent response to the Anthropocene and to understand the presumptions and preconditions that underpin the concept. As discussed, rights of nature represent a minimalist alternative to the status quo and there is plenty of evidence that they can be accommodated by industrial capitalism – even co-existing with petrostates. It may be that no abstract legal concept is sufficient to respond to the powers that are driving the environmental crisis but there is no reason why reform proposals need to exist in isolation from other arguments for radical structural change. With that in mind, I have joined other scholars in arguing for the priority of obligations in response to the Anthropocene. My own argument is grounded in an ethics that is centred around human beings and places emphasis on the source of the problem.

In making this argument, I am not holding out Jonas (or any other theorist) as a panacea for our problems. There are clear limits in his writings and ideas that we would jettison. But we could do worse than enter conversation with a thinker who looked directly into the heart of evil in the 20th century and responded with compassion, and a sense that we could be better than our past suggested. That is exactly the sort of mind-set we need in thinking about future directions for environmental law.

Notes

1 Part of Chapter 4 was first published in "Obligations in the Anthropocene" 31(3) (2020) *Law and Critique*: 309–328. Permission has been granted by Springer (https://www.springer.com).

2 The literature on the crisis of imagination is particularly important to this argument. See for example Haiven (2014) and Fisher (2009).

3 The principles have been reproduced online: https://www.gaiafoundation.org /what-we-do/story-of-origin-growing-an-earth-jurisprudence-movement/ principles-of-earth-jurisprudence/.

4 See for example Cullinan (2011).

5 This is the catchline of the Global Alliance for the Rights of Nature. See for example: https://www.gaiafoundation.org/quito-ecuador-gaia-unites-with -global-allies-at-international-rights-of-nature-symposium/.

6 Moyn (2018: 174) does not appear to accept this reading, arguing instead that the relationship between human rights and neoliberalism were overdrawn.

7 Ecuador's "pay us not to drill" proposal was rejected by the international community but eventually funded by the UNDP. It represented a novel alternative to the countries dependance on oil for GDP. See Keating (2007).

8 This analogy is most pronounced in the United States. See for example literature from the Community Environment Legal Defense Fund: https://celdf.org /2022/04/earth-emancipation-now/.

9 To date, the only development that has engaged the Te Awa Tupua (Whanganui River Claims Settlement) Act (2017) has been the Te Rata Bridge suspension bridge. For details see Clark et al. (2019).

10 Latour (2017: 281) uses the term Gaia. My insistence on using the term "earth system" detracts from his intention which is to describe an intrusion that is transcendent.

11 Weil's objection to rights is primarily that they are rooted in the personal (not the impersonal) and they pit people against one another in an adversarial way Weil (2005: 83) notes: "They evoke a latent war and awaken the spirit of contention. To place the notion of rights at the centre of social conflicts is to inhibit any possible impulse of charity on both sides." For an excellent overview of Weil's writing on rights see Adams (1986) and Hamilton (1986).

12 For a critique of this position see O'Brien (1981).

13 The document can be viewed online: https://www.clarion-journal.com/clar-ion_journal_of_spirit/2010/04/simone-weils-statement-of-human-obligation -1943.html.

14 While Weil is not drawing on Marx it is worth noting that he made the same point. See Marx (1978a: 42): "The practical application of the right of liberty is the right of private property."

15 For broader reflections on this scholarship see Wheeler, Grear and Burdon (2022).

16 For an overview of this literature see Rolston III (2011).

17 In property law the most faithful adherent to this view is Freyfogle (2003).

18 Jonas always describes responsibility and obligations as an option (1996: 108). This means that he does not contravene Hume's law as described in section 2.

Chapter 5

Ecological Integrity[1]

In the introduction to this book, I argued that the Anthropocene requires an active commitment to exercising human power with humility and restraint. In making this argument, I noted that certain approaches to environmental thinking – such as wilderness ethics – are premised on the idea that human beings can step back and allow nature to return to homeostasis. The Anthropocene calls this logic into question by noting that a rupture has been identified in the Earth system itself. As we grapple with this understanding, one thing is certain – the damage we have done to the Earth system exists "at the heart of our lives" and cannot be disavowed (Stengers 2015: 47).

One of the most interesting insights drawn from the Earth systems science is Dipesh Chakrabarty's (2009: 206) argument that the Anthropocene has undercut the "artificial but time-honoured distinction between natural and human histories." The traditional view is reflected in the writing of cultural historian Jacob Burckhardt (1979: 31), who argued that "history is not the same thing as nature" and that history "is the breach with nature caused by the awakening of human consciousness." Here we see the long reach of cartesian dualism in social thought – human consciousness is unique and renders us separate from the environment. Environmental philosophy has long grappled with this idea. Aldo Leopold (1949: 241), for example, was one of the first to push against this logic and tell history in a way that recognised the active role that nature played in human events:

> Many historical events, hitherto explained solely in terms of human enterprise, were actually biotic interactions between people and the land. The characteristics of the land determined the facts quite as potently as the characteristics of the men who lived on it.

More recently, scholars have told history from the perspective of "objects" such as a mushroom (Tsing 2021) or a nutmeg (Ghosh 2022).

DOI: 10.4324/9781003413370-5

Chakrabarty is in conversation with the literature, but I read him as saying something quite distinct: as human beings have become geological agents, our history has converged with the geological history of the Earth (2009: 206). This argument has important implications for environmental lawyers who describe human beings as mere biological agents. Chakrabarty (2009: 206–207) contends that to regard humans as geological agents represents a scaling up of our imagination: "it is no longer a question simply of man [sic] having an interactive relation with nature … Now it is being claimed that humans are a force of nature in a geological sense." Drawing on Chakrabarty, Hamilton (2018: 8) argues that the social sciences "have been built on an understanding of the historical processes that is no longer defensible." As natural history and human history collapse into one another, we must also rethink dichotomies between humans and nature (subjects and objects). This is not interconnectedness in an ecological sense. In the Anthropocene, the human is submerged into the Earth system, and both have more power and volatility.

There are several implications that one can draw from these insights. In this chapter I am interested in how our condition as geological agents blurs the boundaries between human beings and the environment. To be more specific, I am interested in thinking about the extent to which we can say that nature is something "out there" with its own unique integrity. In environmental thought this idea is commonly expressed in the idea of ecological integrity. Like the discussion of rights of nature in chapter four, the concept of ecological integrity is another example of how law has developed in conversation with science and philosophy. Moreover, the concept of ecological integrity can be found in numerous domestic and international legal instruments.

To engage the concept of ecological integrity, this chapter begins by tracing its emergence in philosophy, theology and then in science. This exposition not only clarifies the original meaning of ecological integrity but is important for my argument that the definitional possibilities of concepts are not boundless but marked by their history. Toward the end of this analysis, I argue that in its standard form the concept of ecological integrity is not suitable for thinking about law in the Anthropocene. This is for two reasons: first is the issue of scale. While ecological integrity measures health at the local level, the Anthropocene compels us to think about the Earth as a system. Second, the orthodox concept of ecological integrity remains connected to notions of purity and wilderness which, Chakrabarty suggests, are no longer tenable.

In response to this critique, scholars have begun thinking about the idea of biosphere integrity. This is an ingenious response to the Anthropocene and its proponents argue that it provides a mechanism for measuring the health of one aspect of the Earth system. Rather than thinking about ecosystem health, biosphere integrity is measured with reference to the scholarship on planetary boundaries. Moreover, proponents consciously move away from notions of purity and suggest that biosphere health can be measured with reference to proxies such as genetic diversity and rates of extinction. After unpacking this theory, I turn once again to critique to understand the presumptions that underpin biosphere integrity. Here I argue that the turn to biosphere integrity reproduced some of the concerns with the idea of ecological integrity. Specifically, I am concerned with the retention of the term "integrity" which I don't think can be fully removed from its history. More fundamentally, I argue that biosphere integrity is an idealist discourse that creates an abstraction from reality and is silent on the material causes of the Anthropocene rupture. In this sense, it shares many of the shortcomings of rights-talk explored in Chapter 4.

Intellectual Origins

In the introduction to this book, I argued that many concepts in environmental and ecological law derive from an intellectual engagement with the science of ecology. The concept of integrity enters environmental thought earlier in the context of nascent wilderness ethics. The first reference can be noted in the writing of James Hall who lived in Illinois (US) in the 1820s. Hall's writing evinces a troubling strand in some approaches to wilderness ethics – namely, the affirmation of civilisational progress as indigenous people were displaced from the frontier. In 1828 Hall wrote: "From this land, so lately a wilderness the savage has been expelled; towns and colleges have arisen; farms have been made; the mechanic arts cherished; the necessaries of life abound, and many of its luxuries are enjoyed" (2014: 165). While authors like Nash (2014: 59) have sought to distinguish these sentiments from Hall's writing on wilderness I contend that the two are connected. For Hall, wilderness has integrity not simply because people are absent – Hall was there after all. Wilderness gains integrity once it is cleansed through civilisational progress. This reading is consistent with Hall's subsequent reflections on the industry of the pioneers, which he framed in terms of the "beautiful consummation of that promise, 'thou shalt have dominion over all the earth'" (Hall 1836: 631–632; Nash 2014: 59).

It is in this context that Hall first wrote about the idea of integrity. Reflecting on how settlers had transformed the Ohio Valley "from a desert to a paradise" he noted: "I know of nothing more splendid than a forest of the west, standing *in its original integrity*, adorned with the exuberant beauties of a powerful vegetation, and crowned with the honors of a venerable age." This romantic sensibility celebrated an imagined wilderness which was vast and abundant: "the forest is seen in its majesty; the pomp and pride of the wilderness is here. Here is nature unspoiled, and silence undisturbed" (2014: 54).

Prior to Hall, the idea of integrity was confined to moral and ethical thinking. In this context, the term was used to describe a state of being whole and undivided in oneself. A person had integrity if they demonstrated internal consistency and could withstand hypocrisy.[2] At its most idealistic, the idea of integrity can be linked to purity. I say idealistic because no ancient philosopher held out purity as something that could be fully realised. Part of the human condition meant that we are limited or flawed (something Christian philosophers developed with the idea of original sin). However, no such limitations needed to be placed on the environment – here was a canvass upon which environmental thinkers could project ideas of perfection. This is particularly true in the context of wilderness which was defined through the absence of human beings and the impurities of culture.

The best example is Aldo Leopold's "Land Ethic" which I discussed in the introduction. Here Leopold held that an action is "right when it tends to preserve the integrity,[3] stability, and beauty of the biotic community. It is wrong when it tends otherwise" (1949: 224–225).[4] This is a deontological statement that Leopold used to make further prescriptions about ethics and land management. Two points stand out: first, the land is conceived with respect to wilderness and wild animals. It does not apply to exotic plants,[5] domesticated animals or animals undergoing vivisection (Nash 1989: 71). Those components of the "biotic community" were part of human culture and Leopold does not challenge legal concepts of property and ownership. Second, Leopold did not use the land ethic to argue for the intrinsic value or rights of all wild animals. Leopold himself was a game catcher and his writings are filled with arguments in favour of culling a species once it had exceeded the carrying capacity of the land and risked its "beauty" or the "healthy functioning" of the "biotic mechanism" (1949: 214). For this reason, Leopold's land ethic should not be read as an extension of natural rights from human beings to the environment. His idea is concerned with the good of the whole. If individual biotic value is recognised it is only to the extent that helps preserve the ecosystem (Moline 1986).

From this sketch we can make three observations about Leopold's land ethic: (a) wilderness has its own integrity; (b) that is knowable by ecologists or those close to the land;[6] (c) and which can be preserved through careful management. Integrity in this schema means more than a healthy and functioning ecosystem. It is closer to the idea that here is a balance in nature like homeostasis in the human body. The role of land management is to find this balance through positive actions (i.e. culling) or through withdrawal and preservation. We can extend this final point to say that the land ethic is concerned with the good of the whole and not the individual or component parts of an ecosystem.

Following Leopold, the idea of ecological integrity was developed in two directions – theology and secular ethics. In theology, ecological integrity was interpreted with reference to natural law concepts like human dignity. While scathing of the contribution of Christianity to the ecological crisis, Lyn White Jnr followed Leopold in arguing for the "integrity" of ecosystems. For White, this integrity was knowable through the science of ecology which he felt could provide "new religious understandings of our own being, of other beings, and of being" (1973: 62). White's appeal to integrity was grounded in natural law which he argued derived its authority from God. This was a common perspective which was promoted by the Faith-Man-Nature Groups which sprung up in the United States in the middle of the 20th century (Nash 1989: 103). Daniel Williams, for example, stated simply: "Things have a value and integrity in themselves" because they are part of the "ongoing reality" (cited in Nash 1989: 104). In agreement, Allan Brockway (1973: 37) constructed a "theology for the natural world" which declared that: the non-human world has just as much right to its internal integrity as does the human world, that human beings transgress their divine authority when they destroy or fundamentally alter the rocks, the trees, the air, the water, the soil, the animals – just as they do when they murder other human beings."

Secular environmental philosophy was influenced by these theological currents. This was most evident in the shift from utilitarian conservation and toward the view that environmental protection should be promoted "independent of the usefulness of the nonhuman world for human purposes" (Deville and Sessions 1985: 4).[7] One proponent of this view was John Rodman (1977: 94) who argued that animals and the environment should be respected "for having their own existence, their own character and potentialities, their own forms of excellence, their own integrity, their own grandeur." However, because secular ethics were unbounded from natural law (at least in theory) many scholars also returned to the ethical priority Leopold placed on the whole ecosystem. The most prominent writer in this tradition was John Callicott. Callicott is best read as writing against the grain of the animal rights movement which he critiqued for being "atomistic" in their focus on individual organisms (1980: 324). Against this approach, Callicott argued that the whole had more ethical value than any component part: "Oceans and lakes, mountains, forests, and wetlands are assigned a greater value than individual animals," including human beings (1980: 326).

This is a fundamentally anti natural law perspective because it holds that individual organisms have no absolute dignity that must be respected. While I suspect Callicott would have baulked at the comparison, I read Callicott as sharing important similarities with utilitarian ethics discussed in Chapter 2. All one needs to do is replace the utility principle with holism − an action is judged right or wrong in terms of whether it contributes to the integrity of the comprehensive ecological community. Callicott was consistent in his application of this theory and pushed Leopold's concern with integrity in a new direction. Specifically, Callicott argued that in protection of ecosystem integrity, it may be necessary to prioritise the life of a single endangered or keystone species. He also argued that bacteria and ocean plankton had more ethical importance than human beings (1980: 337).[8] Roderick Nash has observed that Callicott walked back some of these claims toward the end of his career and accepted ideals concerning the value of the individual. This is a tight rope to walk but Callicott does so by affirming that the "health and integrity of the social whole is literally essential to a socially constituted individual's well-being" (1987: 18).

As the concept of ecological integrity was being constructed in the humanities it was simultaneously being developed by ecologists and adapted by policy makers. Far from developing in isolation it is best to think in terms of cross-pollination with each discipline learning and adapting in response to the other. The earliest example can be noted in the *Marine Mammal Protection Act*, H.R. 6558 1972 (US) (MMPA) which was developed in response to the impact that overfishing and bottom trawling was having on marine biodiversity.[9] The original intention of the Act was radical − an absolute ban on hunting or killing marine animals (Nash 1989: 174). However, due to the impact this would have on capital accumulation, the Act was watered down to prioritise the integrity of the marine ecosystem. To achieve this, the Act held that marine animals would not be "permitted to diminish beyond the point at which they cease to be a significant functioning element in the ecosystem of which they are a part." Here the term integrity has been stripped of notions of purity which dominated early philosophical interpretations. But one can see the influence of Leopold's ecological integrity and his contention that the ecosystem has more ethical weight than individual parts. Moreover, consistent with my investigation of legal rights in Chapter 3, one might also view the turn to "integrity" as a way to pacify the more radical demand – that marine life be given individual moral value.

Following the passing of the MMPA, over 80 nations signed the Convention on International Trade in Endangered Species of Wild Fauna and Flora (CITES). The intention of CITES was to create a mechanism for measuring the health and integrity of ecosystems. Rather than measuring each aspect of an ecosystem, the convention used extinction as proxy and established processes for identifying at-risk species. Once classified as at-risk, signatory countries were obligated to restrict trade of the animals and/or associated products. A lot more could be said but for my argument it is important to understand why extinction was used as a proxy for deeper notions of integrity. No doubt pragmatism played a role but there was also deep philosophical reflection. For example, Senator Alan Cranston of California cited Lyn White Jnr to articulate a sophisticated understanding of the way individual organisms contribute to ecological integrity. When a species dies, Cranston noted, "nature has lost one of its components, which played a role in the interrelationship of life on earth." Extinction gives rise to a "void" that can never be recovered (US Congress 1972: 484). This reasoning formed the dominant logic upon which subsequent legislation was based. For example, the Endangered Species Act US (1973) protected not only vulnerable species but also the "critical habitat" on which they depend. For the first time the legislation went beyond federally owned land and applied to private property. For Senator James Buckley, this represented a "quantum jump in man's acknowledgment of his moral responsibility for the integrity of the natural world" (cited in Nash 1989: 177).

While I do not have the space here to highlight every legislative instrument to recognise ecological integrity,[10] another common example cited by proponents is the Clean Water Act US (1972).[11] The legislation empowers the Environmental Protection Agency (EPA) to "preserve and restore the physical, chemical, and biological integrity of the Nation's waters." It is tempting to regard the term biological integrity as distinct from ecological integrity. Does not the former shift our attention away from an ecosystem and toward organisms? However, this is not how the term is defined by scientists. For example, James Karr and Daniel Dudley (1981: 56) defined biological integrity as referring to the capacity of an ecosystem to "support and maintain a balanced, integrated, adaptive community of organisms having a species composition, diversity, and functional organization comparable to that of the natural habitat of the region."

This is similar to the idea of ecological integrity discussed above. However, note that the last part of Karr and Dudley's definition references a comparison to "natural habitat." This is not isolated and has been repeated by many proponents of ecological integrity. Laura Westra (2016: 5), for example, defines integrity as "a valuable whole, the state of being whole or undiminished, unimpaired, or in perfect condition." Due to human impact on natural systems, Westra argues further that "wild nature provides the paradigmatic example of ecological integrity."[12] For a time Karr worked with Westra in the Global Ecological Integrity Group[13] and he developed the Index of Biological Integrity (IBI) as a tool to enable "scientists to provide an approximate description of the extent to which systems deviate from verifiable integrity levels calibrated from a baseline condition of wild nature" (Karr 2000: 96). In the Clean Water Act US (1972), integrity is analysed predominately with reference to the "physico-chemical properties of water" (Capmourteres et al. 2018). However, in other contexts, the IBI attempts to assess integrity by "evaluating the degree to which waters provide for beneficial uses ... water supply, recreational and other uses" (Karr 1981: 22).

What would a generous reading of these statements look like? Unlike Westra, I don't think that Karr should be read as conflating integrity with purity. Borrowing from Holmes Rolston III (2011: 165), I interpret the IBI as attempting to understand the extent to which an ecosystem is dynamic, stable and has a capacity for self-repair with minimal outside intervention. However, as other critics have noted, the IBI makes other assumptions such as the justification for the selection of metrics and the extent to which those metrics can be objectively known (Capmourteres et al. 2018). To this I would add that the choice to place wild nature as the baseline index for measuring integrity is meaningless in the Anthropocene. This is for two reasons – first, as noted in the introduction to this book, the Anthropocene is grounded in Earth systems science which encompasses and surpasses the ecological sciences. Rather than looking back to concepts derived from ecology, environmental legal thinking requires a systematic way of thinking about the new object of the Earth system.

Second, and more fundamentally, if the idea of integrity is to have meaning today it must consider human impact on living systems at the local and global scale. In making this argument I am trying to articulate something more than the common argument that nature includes human beings. I am saying that ecological systems like water are not immune to the rupture of the Earth system which the Anthropocene describes. As Geoffrey Garver (2017: 195) has noted: "The Anthropocene underscores the near certainty that ecosystems completely free of anthropogenic impacts no longer exist—and that widespread human impacts on 'wild nature' have occurred since Paleolithic times." These are facts that proponents of the term need to come to terms with or the word itself should be replaced by something that is more suited to the Anthropocene. I turn now to discuss the most promising attempt to think in terms of the Earth system and also point out limits to this approach.

Biosphere Integrity

In the previous section, I argued that the Anthropocene has made redundant conceptions of ecological integrity which are linked to notions of purity or wilderness. The rupture of the Earth system has fused human and Earth history and there is no place to hide from this reality. Moreover, while ecological integrity has focused at the local and regional level, Anthropocene law requires a mode of investigation that brings the Earth system into focus. It is not a matter of adapting ecological integrity to the larger system – we need a new way of thinking or else the term should be abandoned.

This has led some writers to redefine ecological integrity at a global level and reimagine its parameters for the Anthropocene. The most developed example is Peter Bridgewater et al. (2015: 72) who reconceptualise ecological integrity as a "combination of the biodiversity and ecosystem processes (functions) that characterize the area at a given point in time." Integrity, on this understanding is comprised of the "goods and services" that are required for an ecosystem to maintain itself. This has similarities to the idea of biodiversity health[14] and incorporates animals (including humans) and non-living systems. Moreover, rather than holding on to fixed ideas of purity or wilderness, the authors argue integrity should be measured "at a point of time" to "allow for elasticity in terms of potential change" (2014: 73).

So far, we have an updated version of the concept of ecological integrity articulated above. To respond to the first challenge of scale we need some way to expand the notion of ecological integrity from the local to the planetary. The authors attempt this by noting that the Earth system is made up of component parts that can be brought together to form a whole: "ecological integrity then means the combination of the biodiversity and ecosystem processes that characterize the biosphere as a whole during the

Holocene epoch" (2014: 73). Viewed at this scale, the term "ecological integrity" is no longer appropriate – we have transcended the local community. The authors propose "biosphere integrity" as the appropriate term for Anthropocene scholarship (2014: 73). Just as ecological integrity is measured at a point in time, the authors argue that "biosphere integrity" is measured with reference to the Holocene. The authors to not engage the debate discussed in the introduction about when the Anthropocene started and so we don't have firm dates for this measurement. Instead, the Holocene is chosen because it is "the only state of the Earth System that we know for sure can support contemporary society" (2014: 73).

While the Earth system may be made up of component parts, the authors are aware that the biosphere is also a unique entity and vastly more complicated than measurements made in a local ecosystem. To overcome this issue, the authors attempt to measure biosphere integrity with reference to planetary boundaries (Rockström et al. 2009). The concept of planetary boundaries emerged from an attempt to "identify which of Earth's processes are most important to maintaining the stability of the planet as we know it" and establish what needs to be done "to maintain Holocene-like conditions on Earth, now that we, in the Anthropocene, have become a global force of change" (Rockström and Klum 2015: 59). Johan Rockström and his colleagues identified nine boundaries which if transgressed could result in "linear, abrupt environmental change within continental – to planetary-scale systems." Very briefly,[15] the boundaries are: climate change, changes in biosphere integrity, biogeochemical flows, stratospheric ozone depletion, ocean acidification, freshwater use, land-system change, atmospheric aerosol loading, and the introduction of novel entities. While itemised as separate points of measurement, it is important to understand that each boundary is tightly linked such that if "one boundary is transgressed, then other boundaries are also under serious risk" (Rockström 2009: 474).

Planetary boundaries are a useful tool for thinking about Earth as an interconnected system. We can see, for example, how "significant land use-changes in the Amazon could influence water resources as far as away as Tibet" (Rockström 2009: 474). And yet it is important to note that the boundaries are best conceived guardrails, not tipping points. Steffan (2015b) notes:

A zone of uncertainty, sometimes large, is associated with each of the boundaries … This zone encapsulates both gaps and weaknesses in the scientific knowledge base and intrinsic uncertainties in the functioning of the Earth system. At the "safe" end of the zone of uncertainty, current scientific knowledge suggests that there is a very low probability of crossing a critical freehold or significantly eroding the resilience of the Earth system. Beyond the "danger" end of the zone of uncertainty, current knowledge suggests a much higher probability of a change to the functioning of the Earth system that could potentially be devastating for human societies.

To date, four of the boundaries have been breached: "Two are in the high-risk zone (biosphere integrity and interference with the nitrogen and phosphorus cycles), while the other two are in the danger zone (climate change and land-use changes)" (Rockström 2015b).

The proposal from Bridgewater, Kim and Bosselmann is a compelling restatement of ecological integrity for the Anthropocene. It addresses the problem of scale and, while I maintain that the definitional possibilities for the term "integrity" are not boundless but marked by its history, the authors have distanced themselves from notions of purity. Moreover, by measuring integrity with reference to planetary boundaries, the authors have attached their theory to an internationally recognised method for measuring aspects of the Earth system. I also find laudable the motivation for their restatement – reconceptualising ecological integrity allows us to "leverage" a concept that is "already included in major international instruments in the field of sustainable development" (2015: 74). This is a pragmatic position, motivated (in part) by the magnitude of the crisis and the time frames for responding. And yet, consistent with the other chapters in this book, I also uphold Marx's (1978d: 15) dictum in "For a ruthless criticism of everything existing"[16] that "the work of our time [is to] clarify to itself (critical philosophy) the meaning of its own struggle and its own desires." We must make time for the work or critique, or we risk moving ahead in the wrong direction.

The first stand of my critique is conceptual. Bridgewater, Kim and Bosselmann are fully cognisant that ecological integrity is an elastic idea with varying interpretations. They note, for example, that while ecological integrity is a common term, "there is still no scientific or societal consensus on what it really means" (2015: 64). To resolve this problem, the authors propose that basic elements of statutory interpretation be employed, "using both the letter of international agreements and the apparent intentions of the parties as interpreted through decisions and recommendations" (2015: 68). Of course, this will only get us so far because, as the authors note, the term has been used by a wide variety of parties, for different purposes and with interpretations ranging from "holistic health" and biodiversity. As any law student will attest, it can be hard to determine intention in a domestic legal system, never mind at the global level.

Arguably the connection to planetary boundaries provides some conceptual clarity. As noted above, the term biosphere integrity is one of the nine boundaries that is being measured. I interpret Bridgewater, Kim and Bosselmann as being concerned with this specific boundary rather than as treating biosphere integrity as the culmination of all nine boundaries. If that is the case, it is relevant to note that in their 2009 article, Steffan (2015a) and colleagues did not mention biosphere integrity. This changed in their 2015 article where biosphere integrity was introduced to replace biodiversity loss and includes measurements on genetic diversity. Because Steffan and colleagues were not writing with reference to ecological integrity, it is unsurprising that their theory is different from what has been expressed in ecological law scholarship. Simply put, proponents of planetary boundaries are interested in the specific role that the biosphere plays in the Earth system. They are not treating the biosphere as commensurate with the Earth system. The measurements are also different. Within the literature on planetary boundaries, biosphere integrity is measured in two ways: (1) genetic diversity which "provides the long-term capacity of the biosphere to persist under and adapt to abrupt and gradual abiotic change" (Steffan et al. 2015b); (2) "the role of the biosphere and measures of biodiversity at the global and large biome level" (Steffan et al. 2015b). Naturally, these are complicated measurements with degrees of uncertainty. For this reason, the literature is littered with references to proxies and interim measures until biosphere integrity can be measured with anything approximating efficiency and accuracy (Steffan et al. 2015b).

Conceived in this narrower form, the concept of biosphere integrity may provide a useful tool for thinking about *one aspect* of the Earth system. If, however I have interpreted Bridgewater, Kim and Bosselmann incorrectly and they do intend that their concept of biosphere integrity be measured with reference to the nine planetary boundaries, then that begs a further question – what is their concept adding that is not covered within planetary boundaries scholarship? Put simply, it is the lack of a satisfactory answer to this question that informs the interpretation I have given above.

Finally, there is another aspect of biosphere integrity that demands our attention. That is, the extent to which it reflects an idealistic discourse in the same sense as the analysis of rights articulated in Chapter 4. I have previously argued that there is a fundamental connection between liberal proposals for law reform and philosophic idealism. This involves legislating an ideal/abstract version of a thing (be that a person of the biosphere), which is fundamentally at odds with material reality. Biosphere integrity does not have this idealistic quality when it is being investigated by Earth systems scientists. It is a tool for collecting data and providing decision makers with practical reasons for action. But when it goes from science and into legal prescriptions (i.e., a mandate to retain integrity) then it participates in a similar idealism as rights-talk.

Focusing on ecological or biosphere integrity we might again note the limits of a politics that relies on ideal abstractions. This approach does not name the material causes of environmental harm or engage those forces that course through civil society and render the environment as an object for exploitation. Neutrality to these forces may seem value free but it risks reifying the status quo. To follow Marx (1978a: 32), legal abstractions liberate the state from having to engage the material causes of environmental harm. But individuals still need to navigate those powers on their own and in a depoliticised way. To be more direct, a state may legislate for biosphere integrity rather than addressing extractive capitalism or their own reliance on revenue generated from fossil fuels. The biosphere is legally represented as having integrity but those forces that have caused a rupture in the Earth system may not be addressed. Instead, the state has the freedom to promote integrity through notions of individual responsibility, purchasing carbon credits, denouncing foreign polluters or arguing that they have a moral responsibility to open new coal mines to support the developing world.

A politics that relies on ideal abstractions will always be at some distance from material reality. To repurpose an idea from Wendy Brown (1995: 106), the biosphere is "ideally emancipated" through its promulgation as an abstract entity and is "practically resubordinated" through the idealist disavowal of the material reasons for its active subordination at the level of the economy. Until these material causes of the Anthropocene rupture are addressed, any notion of integrity must be a "narrow," "partial" or perhaps even "devious" form of emancipation (Marx 1978a: 32). In the context of the Earth system, we might ask what an alternative justice claim (or claims) might entail. What other possibilities are disguised by a focus on ideal notions of integrity? And more broadly, what would a focus on materialism look like in the context of the Earth system? I lay the groundwork for this alternative way of thinking in the conclusion of this book.

Conclusion

In this chapter I presented two main arguments. The first is that the concept of ecological integrity is not suitable for thinking about law in the Anthropocene. This is for reasons of scale and its insistence on affirming notions of purity and imagined wilderness. The concept of biosphere integrity addresses some of these concerns by shifting our attention to the biosphere and measuring health at a point of time in the Holocene. However, by way of critique, I expressed concern about the definitional possibilities for the term "integrity" and the extent to which the legal concept of biosphere integrity participates in an idealistic discourse. Because of its abstraction from physical reality I concluded that biosphere integrity does not name those material causes of the Anthropocene rupture. It is this fact that I believe makes it unable to realise its promise.

Having subjected key concepts in environmental legal thought to critique it is time to consider what a materialist approach to the Anthropocene might look like. This is a challenging task because I have argued that liberal approaches to law reform tend to be idealistic in nature. However, I turn now to that task in my final chapter.

Notes

1 Part of Chapter 5 was first published in "Ecological law in the Anthropocene" 11(1–2) (2020) *Transnational Legal Theory*: 33–46. Permission has been granted by Taylor & Francis Group (https://www.tandfonline.com/).

2 For a current definition see (Killinger 2010: 12): "Integrity is a personal choice, an uncompromising and predictably consistent commitment to honour moral, ethical, spiritual, and artistic values and principles."

3 There is debate about whether Leopold included human beings in the term "biotic community." In thinking about this it is relevant to note that human beings were explicitly included in the first formulation of this idea. "A thing is right only when it tends to preserve the integrity, stability, and beauty of the community, and the community includes the soil, waters, fauna, and flora, as well as people" 1947: 52). A lot of ink has been spilled on the significance of dropping reference to human beings in the final version of the land ethic. I regard the omission as significant but for further analysis see Regan (1984: 268ff, 351ff).

4 A similar sentiment can be noted in Thomas Berry's (2000: 17) childhood reflection after observing pristine meadow: "Whatever preserves and enhances this meadow in the natural cycles of its transformation is good; whatever opposes this meadow or negates it is not good."

5 See Elton (1958: 18): "We are living in a period of the world's history when the mingling of thousands of kinds of organisms from different parts of the world is setting up terrific dislocations in nature."

6 I don't read Leopold as holding that only formally trained scientists can know the land.

7 It is not my intention here to set up a dichotomy. Another prominent strand was developed under the banner – enlightened self-interest. Richard A. Watson

(1983), for example, argued that human survival depended on protecting the value and integrity of the environment.

8 Pushing my reading of Callicott further it is interesting to observe that Peter Singer (a Utilitarian) would adopt a similar position in his advocacy of animal rights.

9 For an overview of how the term has been used in multinational agreements and international documents see Bridgewater, Kim, and Bosselmann (2015: 65–66).

10 The literature is vast. Stephen Woodley (2010: 151–152) has noted that ecological integrity is the "most entrenched [term] in the scientific literature, in national and provincial legislation, and in the language of international agreements and treaties."

11 Alongside legislation, see also civil society documents such as the Earth Charter which seeks to "protect and restore the integrity of Earth's ecological systems, with special concern for biological diversity and the natural processes that sustain life."

12 This recent statement is surprising because Westra had previously warned against upholding pure notions of integrity. See for example (Lemons and Westra 1995: 3–4). This is consistent with a trend in Westra's writing which has gradually shifted to more pure statements on integrity.

13 See https://www.globalecointegrity.org/.

14 The authors draw specifically on the UN Convention on Biological Diversity, which defines biodiversity as "the variability among living organisms from all sources including, inter alia, terrestrial, marine and other aquatic ecosystems and the ecological complexes of which they are part; this includes diversity within species, between species and of ecosystems."

15 For full details see https://www.stockholmresilience.org/publications.html.

16 Otherwise known as the Letter to Ruge.

Chapter 6

Materialism in the Anthropocene

This book has been motivated by the concern that strands of environmental legal thought have not encountered the Anthropocene as a paradigm shift that requires us to rethink and, if necessary, abandon concepts developed in the Holocene. To interrogate this concern, I have subjected key ideas to critique – a deliberate practice of trying to unpack the presumptions and presuppositions that underlie an idea, but which are not readily available in the everyday description. It has been important for my project that I have not equated critique with trashing, and I have sought to read scholars in a way that is both generous and productive. This connects to my understanding of critique, which is a generative practice that is directed toward progressing thought so that we may think about law and politics with greater clarity.

The substance of this book critiqued ideas that have become commonplace in environmental legal scholarship. Those ideas are that anthropocentrism is at the root of the ecological crisis and that law reform should focus on proposals for eco-constitutionalism, rights of nature and ecological integrity. With respect to anthropocentrism, I argued that the Anthropocene requires that we accept the perceptual and descriptive forms of anthropocentrism. I also argued in favour of a mode of ethics that is ordered around human beings and material reality. Different critiques were presented in response to the three proposals for law reform but there was a common thread to my critique – namely, the extent to which those proposals are grounded in a politics that presents abstract representations of material reality. I critiqued this approach, not because abstract presentations are bad in themselves. But because a failure to address the material cause of a problem can perpetuate the underlying root cause and affirm the status quo.

While critique has been the dominant method in this book, I am also aware that it is easier to unpack the presumptions of an idea than to propose something new or unique. At the conclusion of this book,

DOI: 10.4324/9781003413370-6

I find myself filled with admiration for those using their creativity to make proposals in what Robert MacFarlane (2019) has described as "our Anthropocene moment." There will never be a flawless proposal or response that is not messy, contingent, hedged and partial. One must, as Donna Haraway (2016) has suggested, "stay with the trouble" and attempt to think through this historical moment as clearly as we can. To this end, I can only hope that the critiques I have presented will help us think about key concepts in environmental legal thought with greater clarity.

For me, the project of critique has highlighted the need for environmental legal thought to be ordered around human beings and engaged in the substance material reality. I do not have a positive legal reform to put on the table to be debated. Instead, I conclude this book by sketching out a method for how legal scholarship might shift from its current preoccupation with idealism and toward materialism. To do this I pick up on a thread of argument noted in the Introduction to this book. Here I noted that the critique of idealism I am applying in this book was first expressed by Karl Marx in his essay "On the Jewish Question" (1978a). Throughout this book I have mined this essay for ideas, modes of analysis and inspiration for ways of seeing. However, it is noteworthy that in "On the Jewish Question" Marx had no alternative to propose. He did not have a critique of capitalism or a notion of what full human emancipation might look like. Nor did he have a theory of social change that was grounded in material reality. The protean spark of such an approach would need to wait until 1845–46 when Marx and Engels wrote *The German Ideology* (1978b).

In this chapter I pick up on Marx's intellectual development and sketch out the concerns for a materialist turn in environmental legal scholarship. The substance of the chapter is a reading of Marx's essay "On the Germany Ideology" where we deepen our critique of idealism and encounter key concepts such as materialism and ideology. My concerns also take me into Marx's mature work and the first volume of *Capital* (1992) which provides a clear example of how historical materialism operates in practice. Drawing on these threads, I sketch out a new direction for environmental legal scholarship in the Anthropocene, which moves away from abstractions and puts in tension a range of factors that are important for social development. Those factors include a concern for technology, our relationship to nature, the processes of production, the ways social life is produced, social relations and our mental conceptions of the world. It should be immediately clear that his framework does not deny the importance of ideas such as normative anthropocentrism. But it does refuse their positioning at the vanguard of change and puts forward a more sophisticated understanding of the range of factors that give rise to our mental conceptions of the world.

Finally, in adopting this approach it is not my intention to advocate for an exclusively Marxist orientation to the Anthropocene. Anyone familiar with the literature will be aware of the burgeoning scholarship that goes under the banner materialism or new materialism (Bennett 2010). This work is using the term "materialism" in a different sense from what is intended here[1] and future work might trace the connections and differences between these fields. It is not my intention to conduct this investigation here except to say that I perceive enough points of connection for a fruitful dialogue. My decision to focus on the Marxist interpretation is justified because of my intersecting interests in a critique of idealism and a mode of investigation that directly addresses a material cause of the Anthropocene rupture.

Materialism and Ideology

As we leave our critique of environmental legal scholarship some big questions have been raised but not answered. First, what is the relationship between idealism (a term I defined as an emphasis on ideas that drive history) and the way the environment is represented by lawmakers. Following Marx (1978a) I have been working on a hunch that liberal approaches to law reform are idealistic and conservative. Abstract representations of the environment allow the state to conserve something of the status quo that needs to be challenged and overthrown. I have made this point repeatedly by noting that neutrality and blindness sound prejudice free. But if extractive capitalism (for example) is a site of social power and a limiting factor in attempts to protect the environment, then for the state to insist on its blindness is to uphold the status quo. In addition to this, we need to have some idea of what is required, for the environment or Earth system to be protected. What does emancipation look like in this context? Thus far, what we have been able to identify as a problem, but not been able to answer, is what is the larger perspective on history that is needed to replace an idealist account? Several answers present themselves, but I want to think about how materialism can provide a counter in which environmental legal thinking can be grounded.

To approach these questions, I propose a reading of "On the Germany Ideology" (1978b) an essay Marx wrote two years after "On the Jewish Question." "The German Ideology" has both a philosophical and a political dimension. German philosophy at the time Marx was writing was steeped in the belief that ideas shape the world and have a kind of power. You change the world by changing consciousness and how things are represented as ideas. We have already encountered this way of thinking several times in this book, i.e., the attempt to define nature as an entity with rights or with integrity. Marx argues that idealism takes root not just in culture but also in politics and law. The tendency in these two arenas is to try and fix social and political problems by talking about them differently, or emphasising changes in the law, rather than reaching into the condition that produces the problem in the first place.

In "The German Ideology," Marx attempts to show that idealism takes hold when you have a particular kind of relationship between the state and society. More specifically, he is trying to show why and how idealism arises from within capitalist society. This is consistent with Marx's approach to history. As he is developing a materialist philosophy, he is going to give a materialist explanation about how idealism arises and why people have such faith in ideas to fix problems. At the same time, Marx is trying to show what he thinks is the right way to think about history and reality. To jump ahead in the analysis, he is going to argue that rich notions of emancipation and liberation can only be achieved through a materialist method, not an idealist one.

With this background in place, we can begin to get into the detail of what materialism entails. To begin, Marx notes that one does not begin with arbitrary premises. Instead, analysis commences with "real premises from which abstractions can only be made in the imagination" (1978b: 149). Thus, we are not starting with abstract ideas about human nature, i.e., we are naturally competitive or cooperative. Marx is going to start by centring the human and thinking about what we do and how we live. How do we produce and reproduce ourselves? How do we engage with the environment and material circumstances of our lives? It is difficult to overstate the significance of this shift in starting point. Hitherto almost everyone in the history of political theory begins their analysis with some abstract idea of human beings. For Aristotle, we are rational animals. For Hobbes, we are desirous and self-interested. For Mill, we are freedom loving beings. What all these ideas share is that they are divorced from material life and the activities human beings engage in to survive.

What do human beings do as a species that is distinct? We produce our means of subsistence by gathering food, building shelters and shaping community. As Marx (1978b: 150) notes: "[humans] begin to distinguish themselves from animals as soon as they begin to produce their means of subsistence." This activity has greater significance than simply sustaining our bodily needs. Marx considers the production of subsistence "a definitive form of activity of these individuals, a definite form of expressing their life, definite mode of life on their part" (1978b: 150). This point is neatly captured in a pithy line: "As individuals express their life, so they are" (1978b: 150). In other words, what we are as a people is developed in coordination with our mode of production – both what we produce and how we produce it.

A lot of things fall out from this starting premise. I will provide a more detailed list below, but examples include the way we relate to others (owners and workers); the tools we use to interact with the environment (technology); our mental conceptions of the world (normative anthropocentrism) and other cultural ideas that are disguised under the veneer of naturalness. For example, agrarian farming communities form types of subjectivity, family, relationality, sexuality, language, literacy, religion etc., just as contemporary forms of subsistence produce those as well. Of course, none of this occurs in a vacuum. How we produce for ourselves depends on what is there already. We are born into an economic order and division of labour and do not have complete freedom over our means of production. To return to a discussion in the introduction, another factor that makes human beings unique is that we are historical animals. Our freedom is bounded, and our material conditions drive history in turn.

From a simple premise – our means of subsistence drives history – Marx has come a long way. It is not necessary for us to trace every branch of his argument in "On the Germany Ideology." Like all his early work, the essay is stuffed with different arguments and lines of inquiry. Rather than thinking broadly, I want to focus in on a single issue: if human life is the product of substance, why does the state represent us in a way that does not correspond to our true lives? To answer this question, Marx introduces the concept of ideology. Ideology has a very particular meaning for Marx. It is a distortion of reality that legitimates the status quo. I have given examples of this in Chapters 3 and 4, i.e., constitutional provisions that say that citizens have a right to a healthy environment or that attach rights to nature. This is ideology (in Marx's use of the term) because neither provision represents reality nor addresses the underlying causes of environmental harm.

So, for Marx, ideas and concepts are woven into the material activity of "real people" (1978b: 154). Human consciousness is always a reflection of consciousness existence. And it is ideology that distorts reality and makes it appear that ideas govern history. To communicate this point, Marx draws an analogy with the camera obscura which was becoming popular in the 19th century: "If in all ideology men and their circumstances appear upside-down as in a *camera obscura*, this phenomenon arises just as much from their historical life-processes as the inversion of objects on the retina does from their physical life processes" (1978b: 154). Put another way, ideology inverts reality and, just like the brain, needs to correct images that come into the head through the retina. The method of critique is required to correct the inverted view of the world that ideology presents to us.

So far Marx has only given us some basic premise of materialism. He is now going to add to those premises three moments in development of materialism itself. Each is important for the argument he is making and understanding how ideology arises. Marx (1978b: 156) starts by talking about basic needs – arguing that "the first historical act" is the production of things to eat, drink, as well as clothing and shelter. These things are not provided to us by nature and require human action and ingenuity. Once basic needs are attained, new needs are created. Human history is always dynamic and always developing. Marx notes: "the satisfaction of the first need (the action of satisfying, and the instrument of satisfaction which has been acquired) leads to new needs." At this stage we might note the emergence of technology (however basic) for efficiency, as well as objects that are individually or collectively owned.

Finally, Marx (1978b: 156) talks about the third historical act where humans begin to reproduce themselves and reproduce their labour: "men [sic], who daily make their own life, begin to make other men [sic], to propagate their kind: the relation between man and woman, parents and children, the family." This process appears like a natural. But Marx puts a different twist on things. He argues that whatever mode of substance develops (and it varies in time and place) produces its own combination or productive and reproductive relations. This is not very difficult to imagine. Consider, for example slave economies where hierarchical notions of race were used to maintain an active form of repression. Another example, which will become important for Marx, is how the industrial revolution rendered the means of production (factories) into the possession of a small owning class, while the great majority were forced to sell their labour in order to meet the basic needs of survival.

What Marx is driving at here is that the mode of production expresses a very particular kind of interdependence or cooperation among human beings, as well as a different model of family, social life etc. And it is the mode of production that is responsible for how those social relations develop. He summarises this point as follows:

> Thus it is quite obvious from he start that there exists a materialistic connection of men with one another, which is determined by their

needs and their mode of production, and which is as old as men themselves. This connection is ever taking on new forms, and thus presents a "history" independently of the existence of any political or religious nonsense which would especially hold men together.

(Marx 1978b: 157)

We can push Marx a little further here to imply a critique of idealism. What holds society together and drives its development is the mode of production and not the ideas or beliefs that individuals or groups within a society hold. This is not a benign situation. There are class interests and politics involved. One aspect of this which Marx focuses on is the division of labour in a society. All societies divide work in some fashion – nobody provides for all of their own needs. Historically, this division goes through lots of phases. But the one that is significant for Marx in terms of understanding where ideology comes from is the division between mental and material labour. Marx (1978b: 159) notes: "Division of labour only becomes truly such from the moment when a division of material and mental labour appears."

Why is this important? Marx is not concerned just with the fact that some people labour and others are telling them what to do. He is trying to understand how mental labour is separated from physical labour in work such as politics and the priest class. In Western history, Marx argues that this division gave rise to three important changes. First, mental labourers will see the world from a particular perspective and things like religion, politics, scholarship will be elevated as the highest value and able to express the truth of humankind. Ideas become the truth upon which everything depends.[2] At this point, Marx argues that consciousness flatters itself about its own independence (1978b: 159). Mental labourers imagine that they are freely thinking about things rather than reflecting the specific histories upon which they find themselves. This is crucial for Marx. Mental labourers think they are getting at the truth, rather than simply reflecting the world that they are in. This is the soil from which idealism emerges. Finally, Marx also says that the division corresponds to a division between rulers and ruled. The ideas of the mental labourers will become the ruling ideas of the age and the mental labourers will dominate.

To summarise, Marx is arguing that ideology is formed when the economically dominant class is also the politically dominant class. In some ways this is obvious and is captured today in ideas like plutocracy. But Marx is making a subtler point: when the owning class are politically dominant, their ideas will become the "ruling *intellectual* force" and ideas will take on an oversized significance in thinking about social development. Marx is also mounting an argument about why a society is going to get a systematic distortion (ideology) when the state and law prioritise ideas as the driving force in history. There is a catch to this as well that I think is implied by Marx's argument. If you don't see the way ideology has been generated, you may just believe that different ideas have dominated at different times because of the power of those ideas. Ideology thus conceals its steps and blinds those thinking about historical development and the best way to impact the future.

Materialism for Anthropocene

In the previous section I sought to understand why idealism has emerged as a governing idea in society today. This is important for my project because I have argued in the chapters above that there is a fundamental connection between idealism and legal scholarship that focuses on law reform. I have critiqued these approaches variously for creating an abstraction from material life and affirming the status quo by not engaging the actual causes of the Anthropocene rupture. "The German Ideology" has been put forward as a text that helps us understand why people think that ideas govern history and why idealism dominates the language in which people express justice claims. As noted, Marx thinks he can answer these questions because a ruling class will conceive of a society based on its interests and perceptions of society. This perception becomes the dominant ideology of the age. The proclamations of the state as it appears in liberal society depend on the conceit that it is ideas that make us free. In response, Marx says that this is a camera obscura or inversion that the dominant class is expressing, and the state is giving voice to in its ideology. The real site of freedom is civil society.

I have presented this reading not because I think the Anthropocene requires a Marxist response. But because I think there is something in the essay that will help us think about a political response to the Anthropocene that is centred around human beings and the material conditions of our lives. This, as I have argued above, is a different way to approach environmental legal thinking than that which currently dominates. Unfortunately for us, Marx did not leave a ready-made plan for how to think about materialism for social change. His work focused largely on the generative possibilities of critique. However, as David Harvey (2010: 189–212, 2011: 126–130) has noted, one can glean from volume one of *Capital* a method for thinking about historical materialism.

The first volume of *Capital* is Marx's most significant work of critique. While never overt, the text can be read as a continuation of his critique of idealism and a focus on the material conditions for historical development. This is obviously a large text and so rather than trace a long argument I want to zero in on a small part of the text which is important for the current discussion. The text is in chapter 15 (1992: 492) during a discussion on the development of machinery and large-scale technology. Marx has already suggested that there can be no such thing as a radical break with the past. The world is not a blank slate upon which a new idea can take hold and grow without reference to the past.[3] In a footnote, Marx offers a short essay where he outlines the various material elements that are active during technological change (in this case, spinning machines). Midway through the essay, Marx (1992: 493, fn 4) notes: "Technology reveals the active relation of man to nature, the direct process of the production of his life, and thereby it also lays bare the process of the production of the social relations of his life, and of the mental conceptions that flow from those relations."

There is a lot packed into that pithy line. Before I unpack it is important to note that the subject that Marx is concerned with is not relevant. What interests me about this sentence is the way it can be broken down and applied to any topic. The key, as Marx goes on to say, is that we need to focus our attention on those "earthly kernels" that explain reality rather than on abstract forms which have become "apotheosized" (1992: 494, fn 4). Returning to the quote noted in the previous paragraph, David Harvey has extrapolated six conceptual elements. They are (1) technology; (2) relation to nature;[4] (3) the actual process of production; (4) the production and reproduction of social life;[5] (5) social relations and (6) mental conceptions of the world. These elements are not static but in motion and linked through a "process of production" that guides human development (1992: 102). Each element can be considered a moment in the process of historical development and is subject to perpetual renewal and transformation.

What does all this mean for environmental scholars thinking about the Anthropocene? It is not my intention to be prescriptive here or to define the parameters of scholarship in my Anthropocene. But I contend that materialism offers a framework for thinking outside of idealism and the limitations of abstract representations of social life. Take, for example, the element relating to our relation to nature. Scholars in the social sciences (and Geography in particular) have long described the ways the environment has been internalised with the capitalist system of production (Smith 2008: 13). For example, Harvey (2014: 247) notes: "The ability of a plant to grow is incorporated ... into agribusiness in its pursuit of profit and it is the reinvestment of that profit that has the plant growing again the next year." The same is true for other aspects of the Earth system – in the Anthropocene all are active agents in the process of capital accumulation. Even the transfer of nutrients in a healthy ecosystem is considered "a flow of value" (Harvey 2014: 247). In part, this reflects neoliberal rationality (as described in Chapter 2) but it is also something that is accounted for in the capitalist mode of production.

We can also use the elements to think about how they relate and blend into one another. This is perhaps most obvious if we combine relation with nature and technology. Some of the most important causes of the Great Acceleration can be traced to the confluence between these fields. Consider, for example, genetic engineering, the creation of new chemical compounds and large-scale environmental changes i.e., the creation of entirely new ecosystems through urbanisation (Smith 2008: 209; Harvey 2014: 247; Calhoun 2013: 152). Human beings are not alone in producing an environment that promotes our future flourishing but today we do so almost exclusively in the name of capital accumulation and without reference to rich notions of obligations. Of course, any exploration of this is also tied to our mental conceptions of the world. Under normative anthropocentrism, human culture (including capital) and the environment are two separate entities in a casual relation. As noted in Chapter 2, many environmental legal scholars think about this relationship in terms of human domination over the environment. In addition, it is also becoming common for scholars writing about the Anthropocene to flip this relationship and argue that it is the Earth system that is taking its revenge on us.[6]

Rather than accepting either dichotomy, a materialist approach encourages us to think instead in terms of perpetual motion and feedback loops. Harvey (2014: 247) captures this idea as follows: "Capital is a working and evolving ecological system within which both nature and capital are constantly being produced and reproduced." This is a unique way to look at the problem and suggests a novel way of thinking about how human impact is interacting with the Earth system. Here I find Marx's process of representation and his idea of "contradictory unity" instructive. Very briefly, when Marx describes a commodity he talks about its use value, exchange value and its value.[7] Each of these terms is held in perpetual and tense relationship and he is concerned to understand how they interact in motion. There is no moment of final resolution or synthesis. But we do see moments where the ideas come together and give rise to new contradictions (or dualities) that need to be explored through further analysis and argument (Harvey 2010: 26). Drawing on this, we might think about the environment as something that is both evolving according to own processes and is being continuously reshaped and re-engineered by the anthropos.[8] Borrowing from Neil Smith (2008: 252), we might in fact say that the Anthropocene is concomitant to the "production of nature" and this is something that can be witnessed "all the way down" to the level of "human bodies for genetic material." In saying this, I am of course conscious that most environmental writers view nature and the Earth system as dynamic and not static. The merit to thinking about these systems in terms of production and motion is that it centres human activity and acknowledges that the direction of change is unknown. This is clear if we look historically, such as the impact of chloro-fluorocarbon refrigeration or at current processes of production which have led us into the Anthropocene.

This is just one example of how engaging with the components identified by Marx may help scholars take a materialist approach to Anthropocene scholarship. As I have tried to model above, the framework allows us to think about human impacts from the perspective of one component or to examine the interactions among them. Taking an idealistic perspective or focusing deterministically on one component as explaining the Anthropocene rupture is insufficient. Thinking into the future will require that we engage across a range of issues that develop unevenly in space and time to produce all manner of local contingencies. In short, we need modes of analysis that capture the complex process between the material causes of the Anthropocene.

Concluding Remarks

This book was motivated by a concern for the direction and future of environmental legal scholarship. On the one hand I perceived that a significant portion of research was not encountering the Anthropocene as a rupture that required us to test, rethink and perhaps abandon ideas that have become orthodoxy. On the other, I was concerned to understand why legal scholarship relies so heavily on the formulation and advocacy or abstract principles or representations of reality. To think about these concerns, I adopted the method of critique which I described as an attempt to bring to the surface the presumptions and presuppositions that underlie an idea, but which may not be readily apparent from how it is discussed or described. My intention in adopting this method was to provide a mechanism that would help us think about common ideas in a new light and from a different perspective. I was also interested in testing the ideas to understand what theory of social change they imply and whether that theory was useful for encountering the Anthropocene rupture.

In conducting this analysis, several conclusions have been reached. First, I argued that the Anthropocene gives us reason for accepting elements of anthropocentrism. More specifically, I argued that one can accept perceptual and descriptive anthropocentrism without adopting a hubristic normativity. While a focus on anthropocentrism is an example of the idealism critiqued in this book, I also provided an updated reading which took into account the economisation of daily life that has become central to neoliberalism. This argument sought to hold in tension the argument against placing ideas at the centre of analysis, while still recognising their role in thinking about the circumstances that have given rise to the Anthropocene.

Following this I critiqued three proposals for law reform: eco-constitutionalism, rights of nature and ecological integrity. These proposals were chosen because of their prominence and influence on environmental legal scholarship. Each critique was unique, but I argued that they all share a commitment to idealism through the presentation of abstract representations of reality. This is never stated explicitly but I argued that idealism is a presupposition that underlies each position. More generally, I argued that liberal proposals for law reform tend to be idealistic in orientation. My main conversation partner in this analysis was Marx's essay "On the Jewish Question." Drawing on this paper, I outlined the limitations of idealism as a politics. Specifically, I argued that idealism tends to maintain the status quo by failing to engage and challenge the material drivers of the Anthropocene rupture.

At the conclusion of this book, I put forward some suggestions of what an alternative to idealism might look like. To do this I returned to young Marx and traced his intellectual development from "The German Ideology" and into his most important work of critique in the first volume of *Capital*. As noted at the start of this chapter, in taking this approach I am not trying to dogmatically advocate for a Marxist approach to Anthropocene scholarship. But Marx has provided me with important tools that have helped me think through the limitations of idealism. In addition, I have looked to Marx for inspiration in thinking about a mode of analysis that is ordered around human power, and that engages the material causes of the Anthropocene rupture. Ultimately, I believe that we need as many approaches as possible to encounter the Anthropocene. That is not to suggest that all approaches are equal or have the same explanatory power; only that our thinking will be better if we allow for a diversity of intelligences and engagements with this most fundamental challenge.

Notes

1 For a discussion see Wheeler, Grear and Burdon (2023).
2 Here it is worth noting that scholars from Aristotle to Arendt placed contemplative man at the apex of human development.
3 This is neatly captured in Saint-Simon's comment: "[n]o social order could achieve changes that are not already latent within its existing conditions" (Harvey, 2005: 1).
4 Marx does not describe this element with specific reference to production. See further Smith (2008).
5 See further Lefebvre (1991).
6 See for example Hamilton (2018: 47): "wherever we look we see human influence, but at the same time we see stirring an 'angry', 'ornery', 'vengeful' Earth that is more *detached* from us that it has been for 10,000 years."
7 It is not necessary for my argument to understand Marx's treatment of the commodity form. But for those interested I have in mind his treatment of the commodity form in Chapter 1. See Marx (1992: 125–128). An example of the duality in a commodity is that it simultaneously has a use value and an exchange value. Either can be the dominant representation at a given point in time
8 As Smith (2008: 253) notes: "Nature is no longer natural, as it were, for all that natural processes continue entirely unabated."

Bibliography

Adams, E. 1986. 'Simone Weil on the injustice of rights-based doctrines' 48 *The Review of Politics*: 60–91.

Agamben, G. 2005. *States of Exception*. University of Chicago Press.

Akchurin, M. 2015. 'Constructing the rights of nature: Constitutional reform, mobilization, and environmental protection in Ecuador' 40(4) *Law & Social Inquiry*: 937–968.

Alves, B. 2022. 'Sales revenue generated by EP petroecuador from 2014 to 2021' *Statista*: https://www.statista.com/statistics/1040376/ecuador-petroecuador-revenue/

Angus, I. 2016. *Facing the Anthropocene: Fossil Capitalism and the Crisis of the Earth System*. Monthly Review Press.

Anker, K. et al. 2021. *From Environmental to Ecological Law*. Routledge.

Ayer, A.J. 2001. *Language, Truth and Logic*. Penguin.

Benson, M.H. and Craig, R.K. 2017. *The End of Sustainability*. University Press of Kansas.

Bentham, J. 1948. *An Introduction to the Principles of Morals and Legislation*. New York Press.

Bentham, J. 1969. *A Bentham Reader*. Pegasus Books.

Bentham, J. 1987. 'Anarchical Fallacies' in J. Waldron (ed), *Nonsense upon Stilts: Bentham, Burke and Marx on the Rights of Man*. Methuen & Coy. Limited.

Bentham, J. 2002. *Nonsense upon Stilts and Other Writings on the French Revolution*. Oxford University Press.

Bentham, J. 2010. *The Panopticon Writings*. Verso.

Bennett, J. 2010. *Vibrant Matter A Political Ecology of Things*. Duke University Press.

Berry, T. 2000. *The Great Work: Our Way into the Future*. Crown.

Berry, T. 2006. *Evening Thoughts: Reflecting on Earth as a Sacred Community*. Counterpoint Press.

Berros, M.V. 2019. 'Rights of nature in the Anthropocene: Towards the democratization of environmental law?' in M. Lim (ed), *Charting Environmental Law Futures in the Anthropocene*. Springer.

Boer, B. 1984. 'Social ecology and environmental law' 1(1984) *Environmental and Planning Law Journal*: 233.

Bonneuil, C. and Fressoz, J.B. 2017. *Shock of the Anthropocene: The Earth, History and Us: The Earth, History and Us*. Verso.

Bosselmann, K. 1995. *When Two Worlds Collide: Society and Ecology*. RSVP Press.

Bosselmann, K. 2014. 'The rule of law grounded in the Earth: Ecological integrity as a Grundnorm' in L. Westra and M. Vilela (eds), *The Earth Charter, Ecological Integrity and Social Movements*. Routledge Press.

Bosselmann, K. 2017. *The Principle of Sustainability Transforming law and Governance*. Routledge Press.

Bosselmann, F.P. and Tarlock, A.D. 1993–1994. 'The influence of ecological science on American Law: An introduction' 69 *Chicago-Kent Law Review*. 847–875.

Boyd, D.R. 2012. *The Environmental Rights Revolution: A Global Study of Constitutions, Human Rights, and the Environment*. UBC Press.

Boyd, D.R. 2017. *The Rights of Nature: A Legal Revolution That Could Save the World*. ECW Press.

Brent, K. 2023. 'Solar geoengineering and the challenge of governing multiple risks in the Anthropocene' in P. Burdon and J. Martel (eds), *The Routledge Handbook of Law and the Anthropocene*. Routledge.

Bridgewater, P., Kim, R.E. and Bosselmann, K. 2015. 'Ecological integrity: A relevant concept for international environmental law in the Anthropocene?' 25(1) *Yearbook of International Environmental Law*. 61–78.

Brockway, A.R. 1973. 'A theology of the natural world' 23 *Engage! Social Action*: 37.

Brooks, R.O. et al. 2002. *The Law of Ecology: The Rise of the Ecosystem Regime*. Ashgate Press.

Brown, W. 1995. *States of Injury*. Princeton University Press.

Brown, W. 2002. 'Suffering the paradoxes of rights' in W. Brown and J Halley (eds), *Left Legalism/Left Critique*. Duke University Press.

Brown, W. 2004. '"The most we can hope for. . . ": Human rights and the politics of fatalism' 103(2/3) *The South Atlantic Quarterly*: 451–463.

Brown, W. 2006. 'American nightmare' 34(6) *Political Theory*: 690–714.

Brown, W. 2009. 'Introduction' in T. Asad, W. Brown, J. Butler and S. Mahmood (eds), *Is Critique Secular? Blasphemy, Injury and Free Speech*. Townsend Press.

Brown, W. 2015. *Undoing the Demos: Neoliberalism's Stealth Revolution*. Zone Books.

Brown, W. 2019. *In the Ruins of Neoliberalism: The Rise of Antidemocratic Politics in the West*. Columbia University Press.

Burckhardt, J. 1979. *Reflections on History*. Liberty Fund.

Burdon, P.D. 2010. 'The rights of nature: Reconsidered' 49 *Australian Humanities Review*: 69–89.

Burdon, P.D. 2014. *Earth Jurisprudence: Private Property and the Environment*. Routledge Press.

Burdon, P.D. 2021. 'On the limits of political emancipation and legal rights' 34(2) *International Journal for the Semiotics of Law*: 319–339.

Burdon, P.D. and Martel, J. 2023a. *The Routledge Handbook of Law and the Anthropocene*. Routledge.

Burdon P.D. and Martel, J. 2023b. 'Mythology for the Anthropocene' in Burdon, P.D. and Martel, J. (eds), *The Routledge Handbook of Law and the Anthropocene*. Routledge.

Burdon, P.D. and Williams, C. 2016. 'Rights of nature: A constructive analysis' In D. Fisher (ed), *Research Handbook on Fundamental Concepts of Environmental Law*. Edward Elgar Publishing.

Calhoun, C. 2013. 'What threatens capitalism now?' in Wallestein et al. (ed), *Does Capitalism Have a Future?* Oxford University Press.

Callicott, J. 1980. 'Animal liberation: A triangular affair' 2 *Environmental Ethics*: 311–338.

Callicott, J. and Lappe, FM. 1987. 'Marx Meets Muir: Toward a synthesis of the progressive political and ecological visions' 2 *Tikkun*: 16–19.

Capmourteres, V., Rooney, N. and Anand, M. 2018. 'Assessing the causal relationships of ecological integrity: A re-evaluation of Karr's iconic index of biotic integrity' *Ecosphere: An ESA Open Access Journal*: https://esajournals.onlinelibrary.wiley .com/doi/full/10.1002/ecs2.2168

Capra, F. and Mattei, U. 2018. *The Ecology of Law*. Berrett-Koehler.

Chakrabarty, D. 2009. 'The climate of history: Four theses' 35(2) *Critical Inquiry*: 197–222.

Chakrabarty, D. 2021. *The Climate of History in a Planetary Age*. University of Chicago Press.

Challenger, M. 2021. *How to be Animal: A New History of What it Means to be Human*. Canongate.

Chami, R et al. 2019. 'A strategy to protect whales can limit greenhouse gases and global warming' *International Monetary Fund*: https://www.imf.org/en/ Publications/fandd/issues/2019/12/natures-solution-to-climate-change-chami

Chomsky, N. 2013. *Necessary Illusions: Thought Control in Democratic Societies*. House of Anansi.

Clarke, C., Emmanouil, N., Page, J. and Pellizon, A. 2019. 'Can you hear the rivers sing? Legal personhood, ontology, and the nitty gritty of governance' 45(4) *Ecology Law Quarterly* 787–844.

Cooper, M. 2019. *Family Values: Between Neoliberalism and the New Social Conservatism*. Zone Books.

Coyle, S and Morrow, K. 2004. *The Philosophical Foundations of Environmental Law: Property, Rights and Nature*. Hart Publishing.

Crutzen, P.J. 2021. 'The "Anthropocene" (2002)' in S. Benner, G. Lax, P.J. Crutzen, U. Pöschl, J. Lelieveld, and H.G. Brauch (eds), *Paul J. Crutzen and the Anthropocene: A New Epoch in Earth's History. The Anthropocene: Politik—Economics—Society— Science*, Vol. 1. Springer. https://doi.org/10.1007/978-3-030-82202-6_4

Crutzen, P. 2022. 'The geology of mankind' 415 *Nature*: 23.

Cullinan, C. 2008. 'If nature had rights' *Orion*: https://orionmagazine.org/article/if -nature-had-rights/

Cullinan, C. 2011. *Wild Law: Protecting Biological and Cultural Diversity*. Green Books.

Dauvergne P. and Lebaron, G. 2014. *Protest Inc.: The Corporatization of Activism*. Polity.

Davies, J. 2016. *The Birth of the Anthropocene*. University of California Press.

Davies, M. 2022. *EcoLaw: Legality, Life, and the Normativity of Nature*. Routledge.

Devall, B. and Sessions, G. 1985. *Deep Ecology: Living as If Nature Mattered*. Gibbs Smith.

Diamond, J. 2005. *Collapse: How Societies Choose to Fail or Survive.* Penguin.

Diggle, J. 2021. *The Cambridge Greek Lexicon.* Cambridge University Press.

Douzinas, C. 2000. *The End of Human Rights: Critical Thought at the Turn of the Century.* Bloomsbury.

Downs, J. 2015. *Sick From Freedom: African American Illness and Suffering During the Civil War and Reconstruction.* Oxford University Press.

Dworkin, R. 1978. *Taking Rights Seriously.* Harvard University Press.

Ecomodernist Manifesto. 2015. http://www.ecomodernism.org/

Ehrlich, E. 1975. *Fundamental Principles of the Sociology of Law.* Arno Press.

Ellis, E. 2012. 'The planet of no return human resilience on an artificial earth' The Breakthrough Institute: https://thebreakthrough.org/journal/issue-2/the-planet -of-no-return

Ellis, E. 2013. 'Using the planet' 81 *Global Change*: 32–35.

Elton, C.S. 1958. *The Ecology of Invasions by Animals and Plants.* University of Chicago Press.

Emerson, A. 1946. 'The biological basis of social cooperation' 39(May) *Transactions of the Illinois State Academy of Science*: 9–18.

Engel, J.R. 2010. 'Contesting democracy' in J.R. Engel, L. Westra and K. Bosselmann (eds), *Democracy, Ecological Integrity and International Law.* Cambridge Scholars Publishing.

Engel, J.R. 2014. 'Summons to a new axial age: The promise, limits, and future of the earth charter' in L. Westra and M. Vilela (eds), *Ecological Integrity, and Social Movements.* Earthscan.

Epstein, S. 2022. 'Rights of nature, human species identity, and political thought in the Anthropocene' *The Anthropocene Review*: https://doi.org/10.1177 /20530196221078929

Erickson, A. 2018. 'Few countries are meeting the Paris climate goals. here are the ones that are' *The Washington Post*: https://www.washingtonpost.com/world /2018/10/11/few-countries-are-meeting-paris-climate-goals-here-are-ones-that -are/

Fader, S. 1979. 'Leopold's some fundamentals of conservation: A commentary' 1 *Environmental Ethics*: 143–148.

Farrelly, C. 2011. Patriarchy and historical materialism. 26(1) *Hypatia*: 1–21.

Farrington, B. 1949. *Francis Bacon: Philosopher of Industrial Science.* Lawrence & Wishart.

Feher, M. 2018. *Rated Agency: Investee Politics in a Speculative Age.* Zone Books.

Fisher, M. 2009. *Capitalist Realism: Is there No Alternative?* O Books.

Fleming, D. 1972. 'Roots of the new conservation movement' 6 *Perspectives in American History*: 7–91.

Fleming, S. 2018a. 'How much is nature worth? $125 trillion, according to this report' *The World Economic Forum*: https://www.weforum.org/agenda/2018/10/this-is -why-putting-a-price-on-the-value-of-nature-could-help-the-environment/

Fleming, S. 2018b. 'How much is nature worth? $125 trillion, according to this report' *World Economic Forum*: https://www.weforum.org/agenda/2018/10/this -is-why-putting-a-price-on-the-value-of-nature-could-help-the-environment/

Francione, G. 1995. *Animals Property & the Law*. Temple University Press.

Freyfogle, E. 2003. *The Land We Share: Private Property and the Common Good*. Shearwater Books.

Fukuyama, F. 1989. 'The end of history?' 16 *The National Interest*: 3–18.

Fukuyama, F. 2019. *Identity: Contemporary Identity Politics and the Struggle for Recognition*. Profile Trade.

Garrett, B. 2020. *Bunker: Building for the End Times*. Scribner.

Garver, G. 2017. 'Ecological integrity in the Anthropocene: Lessons for law from ecological restoration and beyond' in L. Westra, J. Gray and F. Gottwald (eds), *The Role of Integrity in the Governance of the Commons*. Springer.

Garver, G. 2021. *Ecological Law and the Planetary Crisis: A Legal Guide for Harmony on Earth*. Routledge.

Gates, D. 1973. *Biophysical Ecology*. Springer.

Ghosh, A. *The Nutmeg's Curse: Parables for a Planet in Crisis*. John Murray Publishers.

Golder, B. 2015. *Foucault and the Politics of Rights*. Stanford University Press.

Golder, B. 2017. 'On the varieties of universalism in human rights discourse' in P. Agha (ed), *Human Rights Between Law and Politics: The Margin of Appreciation in Post-national Contexts*. Hart Publishing.

Golder, B. 2021. 'From the crisis of critique to the critique of crisis' 92(4) *University of Colorado Law Review*: 1078.

Gonzalez, C.G. 2017. 'Global justice in the Anthropocene' in L. Kotze (ed), *Environmental Law and Governance for the Anthropocene*. Hart Publishing.

Gosh, A. 2022. *The Nutmeg's Curse: Parables for a Planet in Crisis*. John Murray: London.

Grear, A. 2017. '"Anthropocene, Capitalocene, Chthulucene": Re-encountering environmental law and its "subject" with Haraway and new materialism in Louis Kotze' *Environmental Law and Governance for the Anthropocene*. Hart Publishing.

Haiven, M. 2014. *Crises of Imagination, Crises of Power: Capitalism, Creativity and the Commons*. Zed Books.

Hall, J. 1836. 'Chase's statutes of Ohio' 5 *Western Monthly Magazine*: 631–632.

Hall, J. 2014 [1828]. *Letters from the West*. Literary Licensing Company.

Hamilton, C. 1986. 'Simone Weil's 'human personality': Between the personal and the impersonal' 98(2) *Harvard Theological Review*: 187–207.

Hamilton, C. 2011. 'Hamilton: A new brand of environmental radicalism' *Crikey*: https://www.crikey.com.au/2011/02/22/hamilton-we-need-a-new-brand-of -environmental-radicalism/

Hamilton, C. 2013. *Earthmasters: The Dawn of the Age of Climate Engineering*. Yale University Press.

Hamilton, C. 2015a. 'The banality of ethics in the Anthropocene, part 2', *The Conversation*, 14 July: https://theconversation.com/the-banality-of-ethics-in-the -anthropocene-part-2-44647

Hamilton, C. 2015b. 'Getting the Anthropocene so wrong' 2(2) *The Anthropocene Review*: 102–107.

Hamilton, C. 2016. 'The Anthropocene as rupture' 3(2) *The Anthropocene Review*. 93–106.

Hamilton, C. 2018. *Defiant Earth: The Fate of Humans in the Anthropocene*. Allen & Unwin.

Haraway, D. 2016. *Staying with the Trouble Making Kin in the Chthulucene*. Duke University Press.

Harrison, J. 2017. *Saving the Oceans Through Law*. Oxford University Press.

Harvey, D. 1996. *Justice, Nature and the Geography of Difference*. Wiley-Blackwell.

Harvey, D. 2005. *Paris, Capital of Modernity*. Routledge.

Harvey, D. 2010. *A Companion to Marx' Capital*. Verso.

Harvey, D. 2011. *The Enigma of Capital: And the Crises of Capitalism*. Oxford University Press.

Harvey, D. 2014. *Seventeen Contradictions and the End of Capitalism*. Oxford University Press.

Hawken, P. 2007. *Blessed Unrest: How the Largest Social Movement in History Is Restoring Grace, Justice, and Beauty to the World*. Penguin.

Hayward, T. 2005. *Constitutional Environmental Rights*. Oxford University Press EBook.

Heath, M. 2012. 'On critical thinking' 4 *The International Journal of Narrative Theory and Community Work*: 11–18.

Herman, E.S. and Chomsky, N. 1988. *Manufacturing Consent: The Political Economy of the Mass Media*. Pantheon Books.

Hogue, M. 2008. *The Tangled Bank: Towards an Ecotheological Ethics of Responsible Participation*. Pickwick Publications.

Hohfeld, W.N. 1917. 'Fundamental legal conceptions as applied in judicial reasoning' 26(8) *The Yale Law Journal*: 710–770.

Hollo, T. 2022. *Living Democracy: An Ecological Manifesto for the End of the World as we Know it*. NewSouth Publishing.

hooks, b. 2010. *Teaching Critical Thinking: Practical Wisdom*. Routledge Press.

Hume, D. 1960. *A Treatise of Human Nature*. Clarendon Press.

Humphrys, E. 2016. 'Is the term neoliberalism useful?' *Progress in Political Economy*: https://www.ppesydney.net/term-neoliberalism-useful/

Humphrys, E. 2018. *How Labour Built Neoliberalism: Australia's Accord, the Labour Movement and the Neoliberal Project*. Brill.

Jensen, D. 2005. *Listening to the Land: Conversations About Nature, Culture and Eros*. Chelsea Green.

Jonas, H. 1979. *Imperative of Responsibility: In Search of an Ethics for the Technological Age*. University of Chicago Press.

Jonas, H. 1980. *Philosophical Essays: From Ancient Creed to Technological Man*. University of Chicago Press.

Jonas, H. 1996. *Mortality and Morality: A Search for the Good After Auschwitz*. Northwestern University Press.

Jones, D.S. 2012. *Masters of the Universe: Hayek, Friedman, and the Birth of Neoliberal Politics*. Princeton University Press.

Karr, J.R. 1981. 'Assessment of biotic integrity using fish communities' 6 *Fisheries*: 21–27.

Karr, J.R. 2000. 'Health, integrity and biological assessment: The importance of wild things' in D. Pimentel, L. Westra and R. Noss (eds), *Ecological Integrity: Integrating Environment, Conservation and Health*. Island Press.

Karr, J.R. and Dudley, D. 1981. 'Ecological perspective on water quality goals' 5 *Environmental Management*: 55–68. https://doi.org/10.1007/BF01866609

Keating, J. 2007. 'Ecuador: Pay us not to drill for oil' *Foreign Policy*: https://foreignpolicy.com/2007/09/13/ecuador-pay-us-not-to-drill-for-oil

Kelman, M. 1984. 'Trashing' 36(1/2) *Stanford Law Review*: 293–348.

Kennedy, D. 2002. 'The critique of rights in critical legal studies' in W. Brown and J. Halley (eds), *Left Legalism/Left Critique*. Duke University Press.

Killinger, B. 2010. *Integrity: Doing the Right Thing for the Right Reason*. McGill-Queen Press.

Klein, N. 2008. *The Shock Doctrine*. Picador.

Klein, N. 2015. *This Changes Everything: Capitalism vs. the Climate*. Penguin.

Knauß, S. 2018. 'Conceptualizing human Stewardship in the Anthropocene: The rights of nature in Ecuador, New Zealand and India' 31 *Journal of Agricultural and Environmental Ethics*: 703–722.

Kotze, L. 2017. *Environmental Law and Governance for the Anthropocene*. Hart Press.

Kropotkin, P. 2021. *Mutual Aid: An Illuminated Factor of Evolution*. PM Press.

Krugman, K. 2020. 'Apocalypse becomes the new normal' *The New York Times*: https://www.nytimes.com/2020/01/02/opinion/climate-change-australia.html

Kunkel, B. 2017. 'The Capitalocene' 39(5) *London Review of Books*.

Latour, B. 2017. *Facing Gaia: Eight Lectures on the New Climatic Regime*. Polity.

Laval, C. 2017. '"The invisible chain": Jeremy Bentham and neo-liberalism' 43(1) *History of European Ideas*: 34–52.

Lawton, J. 2001. 'Editorial: Earth System Science' 292(5524) *Science*: 1965.

Lefebvre, H. 1991. *The Production of Space*. Wiley-Blackwell.

Lemons, J. and Westra, L. 1995. 'Introduction' In J. Lemons and L. Westra (eds), *Perspectives on Ecological Integrity*. Springer.

Leopold, A. 1947. 'The ecological conscience' *Bulletin of the Garden Club of America*: 45–53.

Leopold, A. 1949. *A Sand County Almanac*. Oxford University Press.

Leopold, A. 1993. *Round River: From the Journals of Aldo Leopold*. Oxford University Press.

Lewis, S.L. and Maslin, M.A. 2015. 'Defining the Anthropocene' 519 *Nature*: 171–180.

Liddle, H.G. and Scott, R. 2005. *A Greek-English Lexicon*. Oxford University Press.

Lilly, S. 2012. *Catastrophism*. PM Press.

Lim, M (ed). 2019a. *Charting Environmental Law Futures in the Anthropocene*. Springer.

Lim, M. 2019b. 'Pathways to equitable sustainability in the Anthropocene: An agenda for legal research', in M. Lim (ed), *Charting Environmental Law Futures in the Anthropocene*. Springer.

Livingston, J. 1994. *Rogue Primate: An Exploitation of Human Domestication*. Key Porter Books.

Loewenstein, A. 2017. *Disaster Capitalism: Making a Killing Out of Catastrophe*. Verso.

Macfarlane, R. 2019. 'Should this tree have the same rights as you?' *The Guardian*: https://www.theguardian.com/books/2019/nov/02/trees-have-rights-too-robert-macfarlane-on-the-new-laws-of-nature

Malm, A. 2015. *Fossil Capital: The Rise of Steam Power and the Roots of Global Warming*. Verso.

Marks, S. 2009. 'False contingency' 62(1) *Current Legal Problems*: 1–21.

Marvier, M. et al. 2012. 'Conservation in the Anthropocene beyond solitude and fragility' Breakthrough Institute: https://thebreakthrough.org/journal/issue-2/conservation-in-the-anthropocene

Marx, K. 1978a. 'On the Jewish question' in R.C. Tucker (ed), *The Marx-Engels Reader*. Norton.

Marx, K. 1978b. 'On the German ideology' in R.C. Tucker (ed), *The Marx-Engels Reader*. Norton.

Marx, K. 1978c. 'The eighteenth Brumaire of Louis Bonaparte' in R.C. Tucker (ed), *The Marx-Engels Reader*. Norton.

Marx, K. 1978d. 'For a ruthless critique of everything existing' in R.C. Tucker (ed), *The Marx-Engels Reader*. Norton.

Marx, K. 1992. *Capital: Volume One*. Penguin.

Matthews, D. 2018. 'Obligations in the new climatic regime' *Critical Legal Thinking*: http://criticallegalthinking.com/2018/07/16/obligations-in-the-new-climatic-regime/

Matthews, D. 2019. 'Law and aesthetics in the Anthropocene: From the rights of nature to the aesthesis of obligations' *Law, Culture and Humanities*: https://doi.org/10.1177/1743872119871830

Matthews, D. 2021. *Earthbound: The Aesthetics of Sovereignty in the Anthropocene*. Edinburgh University Press.

May, J. and Daly, E. 2014. *Global Environmental Constitutionalism*. Cambridge University Press.

Merchant, C. 1990. *The Death of Nature: Women, Ecology, and the Scientific Revolution*. HarperCollins.

Mirowski, P. 2018. 'Neoliberalism: The movement that dare not speak its name' *American Affairs*: https://americanaffairsjournal.org/2018/02/neoliberalism-movement-dare-not-speak-name/

Moline, J.N. 1986. 'Aldo Leopold and the moral community' *Environmental Ethics*: 99–120.

Monbiot, G. 2014. *Feral: Searching for Enchantment on the Frontiers of Rewilding*. Penguin Press.

Moore, J.W. 2015. *Capitalism in the Web of Life Ecology and the Accumulation of Capital*. Verso.

Morris, T. 2013. *Hans Jonas's Ethic of Responsibility: From Ontology to Ecology*. SUNY Press.

Moyn, S. 2012. *The Last Utopia: Human Rights in History*. Harvard University Press.

Moyn, S. 2018. *Not Enough: Human Rights in an Unequal World*. Harvard University Press.

Mylius, B. 2018. 'Three types of Anthropocentrism' 15(2) *Environmental Philosophy* 159.

Nancy, J.L. 2015. 'The existence of the World is always unexpected' in H. Davis and E. Turpin (eds), *Art in the Anthropocene: Encounters among Aesthetics, Politics, Environments and Epistemologies*. Open Humanities Press.

Nash, R. 1989. *The Rights of Nature*. The University of Wisconsin Press.

Nash, R. 2014. *Wilderness and the American Mind*. Yale University Press.

Nietzsche, F. 1989. *On the Genealogy of Morals*, trans. W. Kaufmann. Random House.

O'Brien, C.C. 1981. 'Patriotism and the need for roots: The anti-politics of Simone Weil' in G.A. White (ed), *Simone Weil: Interpretations of a Life*. University of Massachusetts Press.

Odum, E. and Odum, H. 1953. *Fundamentals of Ecology*. Oxford University Press.

Oldfield, F. and Steffen, W. 2004. 'The Earth system' in W. Steffen et al. (eds), *Global Change and the Earth System: A Planet Under Pressure*. Springer.

Proulx, A. 2016. *Barkskins*. 4th Estate GB.

Purdy, J. 2015. *After Nature: A Politics for the Anthropocene*. Harvard University Press.

Pyne, S.J. 2021. *The Pyrocene How We Created an Age of Fire, and What Happens*. University of California Press.

Raff, M. 2003. *Private Property and Environmental Responsibility: A Comparative Study of German Real Property Law*. Kluwer Law International.

Rawls, J. 2000. *Lectures on the History of Moral Philosophy*. Harvard University Press.

Raz, J. 1986. *The Morality of Freedom*. Cambridge University Press.

Regan, T. 1984. *Earthbound: New Introductory Essays in Environmental Ethics*. Random House.

Rickards, L. 2017. 'Defiant earth: The fate of the humans in the Anthropocene' *Australian Book Review*: https://www.australianbookreview.com.au/abr-online/archive/2017/212-october-2017-no-395/4297-lauren-rickards-reviews-defiant-earth-the-fate-of-the-humans-in-the-anthropocene-by-clive-hamilton

Robin, C. 2016. 'How intellectuals create a public' *The Chronicle*: https://www.chronicle.com/article/how-intellectuals-create-a-public/

Robinson, N.A. 2020. 'Making environmental law function in the Anthropocene' 50(6) *Environmental Policy and Law*: 471–477.

Rockström, J. 2015. 'Bounding the planetary future: Why we need a great transition' Great Transition Initiative, April 1. http://www.greattransition.org/publication/bounding-theplanetary-future-why-we-need-a-great-transition.

Rockström, J. and Klum, M. 2015. *Big World, Small Planet: Abundance within Planetary Boundaries*. Yale University Press.

Rockstrom, J. et al. 2009. 'A safe operating space for humanity' 461 *Nature*: 472–475.

Rodman, J. 1977. 'The liberation of nature?' 20 *Inquiry*: 94–101.

Rolston III, H. 1989. *Philosophy Gone Wild: Environmental Ethics*. Prometheus Books.

Rolston III, H. 2011. *A New Environmental Ethics: The Next Millennium for Life on Earth*. Routledge.

Ruddiman, W.F. 2003. 'The Anthropogenic greenhouse era began thousands of years ago' 61 *Climate Change*: 261–293.

Saito, K. 2017. *Karl Marx's Ecosocialism: Capital, Nature, and the Unfinished Critique of Political Economy*. Monthly Review Press.

Schofield, P. 2006. *Utility and Democracy: The Political Thought of Jeremy Bentham*. Oxford University Press.

Seed, J. 2007. *Thinking Like a Mountain: Towards a Council of All Beings*. New Catalyst Books.

Sessions, G.S. 1974. 'Anthropocentrism and the environmental crisis' 2(1) *Social Behaviour and Natural Environments*: 73.

Shapiro, S. 2011. *Legality*. Harvard University Press.

Shaw, M. 2021. 'Billionaire capitalists are designing humanity's future. Don't let them', 5 February, *The Guardian*: https://www.theguardian.com/commentisfree/2021/feb/05/jeff-bezos-elon-musk-spacex-blue-origin

Siedentop, L. 2017. *Inventing the Individual: The Origins of Western Liberalism*. Belknap Press.

Simons, H.C. 1941. 'For a free-market liberalism' 8(2) *University of Chicago Law Review*: 202–214.

Singer, J.W. 2000. *Entitlement: The Paradoxes of Property*. Yale University Press.

Singer, P. 1981. *The Expanding Circle: Ethics, Evolution, and Moral Progress*. Oxford University Press.

Smee, B. 2018. Domestic tourism to Great Barrier Reef falls in wake of coral bleaching. *The Guardian*: https://www.theguardian.com/environment/2018/jun/08/domestic-tourism-to-great-barrier-reef-falls-in-wake-of-coral-bleaching

Smith, B.D. and Zeder, M. 2013. 'The onset of the Anthropocene' 4 *Anthropocene*: 8–13.

Smith, N. 2008. *Uneven Development: Nature, Capital, and the Production of Space*. University of Georgia Press.

Sparrow, J. 2021. *Crimes Against Nature: Capitalism and Global Heating*. Scribe.

Steffen, W. et al. 2004. *Global Change and the Earth System: A Planet Under Pressure*. Springer.

Steffen, W. et al. 2015a. 'The trajectory of the Anthropocene: The great acceleration' 2(1) *The Anthropocene Review*: 81–98.

Steffan, W. et al. 2015b. 'Planetary boundaries: Guiding human development on a changing planet' 437(6223) *Science*. https://doi.org/10.1126/science.1259855

Stengers, I. 2015. *In Catastrophic Times: Resisting the Coming Barbarism*. Open Humanities Press.

Stone, C.D. 1972. 'Should trees have standing?: Toward legal rights for natural objects' 45 *Southern California Law Review*: 450–501.

Stone, C.D. 2010. *Should Trees Have Standing?: Law, Morality, and the Environment*. Oxford University Press.

Taylor, P., Don, B. and Burdon, P.D. 2020. 'Moral leadership and climate change policy: The role of the world conservation union' 23(1) *Ethics, Policy and Environment*: 1–21.

Telesetsky, A., Cliquet A. and Akhtar-Khavari, A. 2019. *Ecological Restoration and International Environmental Law*. Routledge Press.

Tsing, A. 2021. *The Mushroom at the End of the World: On the Possibility of Life in Capitalist Ruins*. Princeton University Press.

Turgut, N.Y. 2008. 'The influence of ecology on environmental law: Challenges to the concept of traditional law' 10(2) *Environmental Law Review*: 112–130.

U. S. Congress. 1972. 'Subcommittee on fisheries and wildlife conservation: Hearings, predatory mammals and endangered species' in 92d Congress, 2d session.

Valencia, A. 2022. 'Ecuador's state oil company looks to double output in five years' Reuters: https://www.reuters.com/business/energy/ecuadors-state-oil-company-looks-double-output-five-years-2022-03-11/

Vermeylen, S. 2017. 'Materiality and the ontological turn in the Anthropocene: Establishing a dialogue between law, anthropology, and eco-philosophy' in L. Kotze (ed), *Environmental Law and Governance for the Anthropocene*. Hart Publishing.

Wark, M. 2016. *Molecular Red: Theory for the Anthropocene*. Verso.

Washington, H. et al. 2021. 'The trouble with Anthropocentric Hubris, with examples from conservation' 1 *Conservation*: 285–298.

Watson, R.A. 1983. 'A critique of anti-Anthropocentric biocentricism' 5 *Environmental Ethics*: 245–256.

Weil, S. 1943. 'Draft for a statement of human obligation' https://www.clarion -journal.com/clarion_journal_of_spirit/2010/04/simone-weils-statement-of -human-obligation-1943.html

Weil, S. 2001. *The Need for Roots*. Routledge.

Weil, S. 2005. 'Human personality' in *Simone Weil: An Anthology: An Anthology*. Penguin.

Westra, L. 2016. *Ecological Integrity and Global Governance: Science, Ethics and the Law*. Routledge Press.

Wheeler, W.M. 1926. 'Emergent evolution of the social' 64(November 5) *Science*: 433–440.

Wheeler, S., Grear, A., and Burdon, P. 2023. 'Law, responsibility and the Capitalocene: In search of new arts of living' in P. Burdon and J. Martel (eds), *The Routledge Handbook of Law and the Anthropocene*. Routledge.

White, L. 1967. 'The historical roots of our ecological crisis' 155(3767) *Science*: 1203.

White, L 1973. 'Continuing the conversation' in I.G. Barbour (ed), *Western Man and Environmental Ethics*. Longman Higher Education.

White, L. 2012. 'Intervene, I said' *Overland Journal*: https://overland.org.au/previous -issues/issue-207/feature-jessica-whyte/

Whyte, J. 2019. *The Morals of the Market: Human Rights and the Rise of Neoliberalism*. Verso.

Woodley, S. 2010. 'Ecological integrity and Canada's National Parks' 27 *George Wright Forum*: 151–160.

Yusoff, K. 2018. *A Billion Black Anthropocenes of None*. University of Minnesota Press.

Zalasiewicz, J. et al. 2017. 'The working group on the Anthropocene: Summary of evidence and interim recommendations' 19 *Anthropocene*: 55–60.

Index

Printed in the United States
by Baker & Taylor Publisher Services